10\90

3000 800022 57254
St. Louis Community College

D1271148

WITHDRAWN

 St. Louis Community College

Forest Park
Florissant Valley
Meramec

Instructional Resources
St. Louis, Missouri

St. Louis Community College
at Meramec
Library

CINEMA CLASSICS

A facsimile reprint series of significant books
on film history, and film criticism, including
a number of important screenplays

Selected by
The American Film Institute
Louis B. Mayer Library

A Garland Series

George Stevens

An American Romantic

Donald Richie

Garland Publishing, Inc.
New York & London   1985

For a complete list of the titles in this series
see the final pages of this volume.

Reprinted by permission of The Museum of Modern Art
© The Museum of Modern Art, 1970

Library of Congress Cataloging in Publication Data

Richie, Donald, 1924—
   George Stevens, an American romantic.

   (Cinema classics)
   Reprint. Originally published: New York : Museum of
Modern Art, 1970.
   1. Stevens, George Cooper, 1904—   . I. Title.
II. Series.
PN1998.A3S8   1984   791.43'0233'0924   82-49211
ISBN 0-8240-5773-2   (alk. paper)

Design by Donna Montalbano

The volumes in this series are printed on
acid-free, 250-year-life paper.

Printed in the United States of America

George Stevens
An American Romantic
by Donald Richie

The Museum of Modern Art, New York

Distributed by New York Graphic Society Ltd.
Greenwich, Connecticut

Cover: Montgomery Clift and Elizabeth Taylor in *A Place in the Sun*

© The Museum of Modern Art, 1970
11 West 53 Street, New York, N.Y. 10019

Library of Congress Catalog Card Number 68–54916

Designed by Michael Lauretano

Filmography by Melinda Ward and Regina Cornwell

Photographs courtesy of The Museum of Modern Art Film Library and George Stevens

Type set by Westcott & Thomson, Inc., Philadelphia, Pa.

Printed and bound by Eastern Press, Inc.,
New Haven, Conn.

Following page: *Shane*

George Stevens is one of America's most honored directors. A man who has always honestly tried to please his audience, he has been singularly successful. The audiences of *Alice Adams, Gunga Din, Shane,* loved these films. They recognized themselves in them.

Stevens' film world is, in this way, larger than the body of pictures which he created. Few directors have, through sharing the assumptions of their audiences, proved more of their place and era. To speak of the life and work of George Stevens is to speak of his life and times.

This, the first monograph on Stevens, is one long due. It represents an attempt to situate him rightly, to provide the context of his work, and to see throughout the course of his long career something that is pertinent to America during these times.

Whether or not he intended such a thing, Stevens has, in a very important way, become the spokesman for his country and his decades. His work, as he moved from craftsman to artist, from romantic to realist, reflects the course of the nation, and those assumptions, both social and philosophical, upon which it is based. Technically his films are characterized not only by brilliant use of the camera, but also by great sensitivity for the relationship between music and the visual flow of his images. Unlike many younger directors, he knows and controls every aspect of his craft. To look again at *A Place in the Sun* is a revelation. The perfect matching of technique to the requirements of the script is the mark of a master craftsman.

Willard Van Dyke
Director, Department of Film

Romanticism will exist in human nature
as long as human nature itself exists.
The point is . . . to adopt that form of romanticism
which is the mood of the age.

Thomas Hardy, *Journal,* 1880

The individual, right or wrong. This is the traditional American attitude. It is also the traditional romantic attitude. Reality is subjective. This is the view of a person who has discovered that what he feels about something is more important than what he thinks about it. These feelings—he decides—create his individuality.

Romantics, European and American, evaluate reality and find it wanting. They feel that it should be, somehow, ideal; closer, somehow, to their feelings of what ought to be. To this end, romantics write manifestoes, create social contracts, or engross themselves in realizing the American dream.

The attitude is one of optimism. The American pioneer, an individual in the wilderness, thought he was making a better life, a finer society. He believed in the ability of man to progress, and in the possibility of a better world. His assumption, one he shared with romantics the world over, was that there is something innately good in man; that, no matter how he might be perverted by this imperfect world, this core of virtue remained.

George Stevens, born in Oakland, California, in 1904, like most Americans of his time, was heir to these assumptions. They consisted, in part, of optimism, faith in innate good, liberalism toward other individuals, and belief in the absolutes of truth and beauty. Like most Americans, he was a romantic, an idealist.

That he did not so remain has become apparent. Eventually he began to question these assumptions, so central to the American experience. As he turned from movie craftsman into film artist, as he came to realize that cinema is an entertainment which is also an art, he became less typical; he turned into a true individual. The career of George Stevens is, thus, also the history of a philosophy—one which he initially shared with the majority of his contemporaries.

Simple optimism, idealism, is part of romanticism, but not all of it. The romantic knows that reality is, perhaps unfortunately, different from his subjective feelings of what it should be. Stevens came to this realization early in his career, and sought a number of ways to circumvent the difficulty. He tried to create a world where the romantic individual achieved all of his dreams; conversely, he tried to show this individual that the horrors of the actual world were not really that bad. It was only in his later pictures, and as he was maturing as an artist, that he realized that circumvention is not possible, that the problems the romantic faces in the world are real and not to be dismissed. Rather, he learned, the problem—that of an individual in a society—must be faced, and that the acceptance of the problem, the determination of the individual to confront himself in his place in this world, led to no single conclusion, but to a heightened and deepened acceptance of the problems of life itself.

Initially, however, Stevens was no different from any of the American romantics making movies in the 1930s. In the early comedies and westerns that Stevens photographed and helped direct, in his own first full-length films—Wheeler and Woolsey comedies, light romances— there seems to be no doubt that all is well with the world. As early as the 1935 Laddie, however, and certainly by the time of Alice Adams, completed in the same year, Stevens showed that something was wrong.

He had discovered the great romantic theme of the individual and his society, the plight of this individual

Laddie. John Beal, center

Fred MacMurray and Katharine Hepburn in *Alice Adams*

in a nation of presumed individuals, the needs of the individual whose society has no place for him. This, already a theme in European literature, had become the major theme in American literature, extending now from the romances of Charles Brockden Brown through *Portnoy's Complaint.* As the common intellectual currency of America, it has been used by many film directors before and since Stevens. Only he, however, has made it so peculiarly his own, by following its assumptions to their conclusion, by exposing their roots.

Alice Adams lives in the small and typically American town of South Renford. Coming from a lower-middle-class family, she is ashamed of her clothes, of her house, of the fact that her brother has to take her to the dances given by those wealthier. Very much the individual, she has her own way of dressing, talking, thinking. These combine to make her unpopular with those who have less individuality than she. When a wealthy young man, the local catch, pays attention to her, he does so because he sees this individuality which small-town society has not yet stifled.

This society is much like that seen in the novels of Sinclair Lewis, though of an earlier period. Already the initial version of the American dream is fading. The rich live on one side of the tracks, the poor on the other; the innate good of the former is being smothered, that of the latter is being attenuated. There is no place for the individual who feels that, somehow, the world ought be a better place than it is.

This is the milieu of *Main Street*—a novel that would have suited the young Stevens admirably—and Alice is just as fierce an individualist as Carol Kennicott, the heroine of the Lewis book. She feels that she embodies standards of truth and beauty, and fights to retain them. She is successful. Seeing her goodness, the young man proposes. The poor girl turned rich, the outcast turned leader of her society, she reconciles within herself the unfortunate social schism that prevented the world from being the place it should have been. From now on, for her at least, it will be.

In the Booth Tarkington novel on which the picture is based, Alice is not successful. The boy does not propose. Rather, Alice decides to go to a secretarial school and forget all this nonsense. But then Tarkington's novel is not romance but social realism. He sees that Alice is wrong—that she is affected, and even more snobbish than the society that excludes her. She is obviously a misfit, but this is cause for complaint rather than rejoicing. Toward the end of the novel she begins to mature; she will make a good secretary.

The differences between novel and film are basic. Stevens, although concerned with the feelings of the misunderstood individual, did not wish to see that an alternative for his heroine's unhappiness might possibly lie in having her change her ways. Today he would. If Stevens were to remake *Alice Adams*, he would agree with Tarkington. He would not, at any rate, settle for the happy miracle that concludes this as well as many another romantic novel and film.

At the time, however—and even granting the pressures of production companies and their ideas of their audience—this was one of the ways Stevens chose to solve the problem of an individual desperate in a society not yet utopian.

Another way—one to which Stevens never succumbed —was to give up trying. Unable to discover the best, one willingly finds the worst. Disillusion is expressed rather than optimism—these two qualities being close, and indifference being their true opposite. Idealism is inverted, and cynicism takes the place of faith. There are a number of examples among film directors—that of Billy Wilder being perhaps the best known.

Yet another possibility, and one seen in the later work of Stevens, is to give up the happy ending, the easy resolution—to admit that the root of the problem is not the social schism, that it is more complicated than that. To be a true individual one must insist upon his individuality and define it. One is responsible for oneself and one's beliefs. This is the resolution of the romantic theme, and one finds it in Stevens' postwar films. Yet, the theme remains the same. First sounded in the person of Alice Adams, it is heard in all of its richness and complexities through George Eastman, Shane, Jett Rink, and Jesus Christ.

"A fine romance, my friend, this is . . . ."
—*Swing Time*

Early in his career, Stevens had begun to question the assumptions to which he had been born heir—an activity by no means as rampant then as it is now. In seeking to present this director through his themes and his illustration of them, one sees that this early awareness of an imperfect world indicates an enormous and completely vulnerable sensitivity which sought in several ways to evade painful issues before it finally faced them. One finds also a kind of courage, often baffled though it was, which continued to probe more and more deeply into the problems it found central to our place and time. Stevens has sometimes been dismissed as a sentimentalist, as a carpenter interested mainly in public acceptance of his carpentry, as an old-fashioned idealist. None of these charges is true, although he is an excellent craftsman, always films for his audience, has been idealistic, and has certainly often enough been sentimental. These charges are not true because they are not all. George Stevens is more than this, and this became increasingly evident during his career.

No matter the pressures of producers, writers, actors, Stevens did choose his vehicles and hence his themes. A man is what he does, after all. His past actions and past creations define him. There is no such thing as a man's being made to do something against his will, because, if he does it, no matter what the pressures, then he wanted to do it more than he wanted not to do it.

Stevens is as responsible for *Something to Live For* as he is for *A Place in the Sun,* regardless of the absurdities or excellences of each. It was he who chose to do, or, at least, did not choose not to do them.

In the same way, he chose, very early in his career, the romantic theme which became so securely his. This theme, this attitude, represents a choice. It is possible for everyone to observe both objectively and subjectively, just as it is possible for everyone to feel and to think. To choose but one, rather than both, is already romantic.

And we commonly make such a choice. Now—even particularly now—we opt for feeling over thought. This choice is so American that it is taken for granted. That Stevens even concerns himself with the results of this choice infuriates his critics. They criticize in him an obviousness, a lack of imagination, that fish in a pond

14

might lavish upon their single member who is interested in the nature of water.

Early having seen that his philosophical heritage was not sufficient to cope with the problems encountered in a startlingly imperfect world, Stevens—probably without deciding, certainly without talking about it—began casting about for solutions, since he still believed a solution possible.

One of the first solutions lay in forcing an assumption. Even if the world is wanting, the innately good will somehow prevail. This kind of solution resulted in a number of happy-ending films: *Alice Adams, Annie Oakley, Quality Street, Penny Serenade, Woman of the Year,* even—if one agrees that the ending was eventually happy—*The Greatest Story Ever Told.* But ultimately, this was no solution. One refuses to believe in these happy endings; one even doubts that Stevens did. The resolutions are so facile that even the enormous amounts of emotion that the director was able both to create and command cannot carry conviction out of the theater and into the street.

Another solution—one that Stevens thoroughly explored before giving it up, and one to which American artists are particularly prone—is to admit that the present is imperfect, that the utopian future is unlikely, but that the past was certainly golden. Even if present and future must be relinquished, the past is firmly in hand. One compromises.

Gunga Din, Quality Street, Annie Oakley, I Remember Mama, are all, in their separate ways, evocations of a golden past. So, to an extent, are *Shane* and *Giant,* although these are much more complicated pictures in that their past is directly connected to our present.

Barbara Bel Geddes as Katrin in *I Remember Mama* is a younger and different version of Katharine Hepburn in *Alice Adams*. She knows that the family is poor and that the injustices of this world are great. She also knows, however, that there is a solution other than the either/or choice of happy marriage with the local rich boy as contrasted with the horrors of life at home.

Specifically, she finds the promise of a better world in the evocation of a past one. As the film opens, she has just finished rereading her novel about her family. Closing the manuscript, she allows her mind to wander back over the past (as Stevens' heroines sometimes do: Irene Dunne plays phonograph records while remembering most of *Penny Serenade*). There are Mama Irene Dunne, Papa Philip Dorn, Uncle Oscar Homolka, all moving through the pages of the book and reels of the film just as though they were alive.

Like a San Francisco Proust, Barbara has discovered that the past recaptured allows the thwarted romantic a backward glance that reassures. What once seemed chaos falls into patterns, and one may conclude that the muddled present will likewise be clarified. Unlike Proust, however, Barbara and her director are content to stop there.

Neither of them, therefore, need concern himself with the fact that the patterned past is dead, that this imagined perfection is perfect only because death is always perfect and life is always imperfect. "Oh, she never looked more beautiful," people sometimes say while viewing a cadaver. And they are right. Death, eternal being and the end of becoming, is the closest we ever come to perfection.

This apprehension causes some artists to become

death haunted. In literature one traces a development from Hawthorne, through Poe, through Faulkner, to any number of younger romantic writers. The same is true in American cinema. Murnau is a close example; Robert Aldrich with his sensationally macabre is an almost ludicrously apt one. Stevens, however, remained too optimistic to find this solution attractive. Also, he found in his later films new uses for the past, and new uses for the character who would put his past in order and finally admit its consequences.

This early in his career, however, with his romantic's apprehension that all was not well with the world, and his romantic's duty to do something about it, he attempted to find other compromises.

"Noise? That's swing. It's time the old place was brightened up a little."
—*A Damsel in Distress*

Lady Constance Collier remonstrates, but Lord Montagu Love snaps his fingers, wags his head, shakes his forefinger, when the old English madrigal breaks down as Fred Astaire takes over the drums for a hot rhythm number.

Again, in *Woman of the Year,* Katharine Hepburn, an intellectual given to foreign languages and political economy, is taken by Spencer Tracy to a ball game. In no time she is on her feet, caught up in the game. Fists clenched, hat awry, she yells at the batter: "Come on, Joe!"

Or, in *Vivacious Lady,* Beulah Bondi has gone to talk to the errant lovers. Shortly after, they endeavor to teach her the latest dance sensation, the Big Apple.

James Ellison, Beulah Bondi and Ginger Rogers in *Vivacious Lady*

At first hesitant, even disapproving, the dignified old lady bit by bit loses her inhibitions, begins waving her hands, turning her ankles, shaking her bottom. The young people smile as they gyrate. Mother's gotten hot, she's gotten with it.

Such scenes, and others like them, are relished, are stretched out long. One reason is the audience's presumed enjoyment, a quality to which Stevens was never indifferent. Another is that they indicate another compromise, perhaps a way out of the romantic dilemma.

The romantic individual, a believer in absolutes and given to subjective feelings about the world, finds himself in a society that is not interested in his emotional problems, and one, further, in which values are merely relative. It is a hard lot. Why not just give up? After all, you're only young once.

Thus, to get hot, or to get with it, means to join the party; to realize, after all these years, that something is fun; that one has been an old fogey perhaps, but that it's never too late. The examples above indicate the direction, but they are not the richest of Stevens' illustrations of the compromise.

One such occurs in *The Talk of the Town*. Ronald Colman is "a number-one legal genius [who] eats with the governor, writes to the president." Cary Grant, on the other hand, has not had much book-learning, but he is a real man of the common people. He knows through practice in the arena of life what Professor Colman in his ivory tower knows only in theory. Consequently, the number-one legal genius soon comes to see the error of his ways. Softened up by that great spiritual tonic, a real American baseball game, carried away by enthusiasm for his new-found oneness with the Amer-

Joan Fontaine and Fred Astaire in *A Damsel in Distress*

Ronald Colman, Jean Arthur and Cary Grant in *The Talk of the Town*

ican people, he is ready for a salutary action. He shaves off his beard, symbol of difference and distinction. The sound track briefly carries the triumphant opening measures of the third-act prelude of *Lohengrin.* Colman dashes on the lather, dashes off the beard. A man of mere contemplation has become a man of action, and this is good.

Colman's specialty, incidentally, was eighteenth-century law, that classical study extending from a time when individuality was continually subverted to the needs of a stabilized society. Grant is a kind of populist. Unlettered, but making up for this lack by innate folk wisdom and deep feelings, he represents—as though in a historical allegory—the romantic revolt itself. Their opposition is, in microcosm, the intellectual history of the past several hundred years.

Classicism loses. Colman shaves off his beard. His abandonment of his standards, his relinquishing of the entire intellectual apparatus of the law, are small sacrifices to the greater good of his so joyfully entering our common pond.

The giving up of all intellectual standards is, of course, a part of the romantic repertoire. Though we no longer think particularly well of young men killing themselves in despair, of young ladies jumping off heights (both actions indicative of desperate but somehow laudable emotional states resulting in a loss of standards as well as life itself), we still retain the belief that something one feels is somehow more real than something one merely thinks. That emotions are only ideas is in itself an idea which, when it occurs, marks the end of romanticism and the beginnings of something else.

In this abandoning of standards one rescues the feeling of hope of a better world, although hopes of doing something about the world are abandoned. It is as if Alice Adams had suddenly come to recognize that the stuffy folks on the better side of the tracks were not so bad after all, that they had their good points just like everyone else, and, anyway, it is differences that make the world go round.

That the solution itself is romantic is indicated by its either/or quality. It does not occur to Alice just to take that course in the secretarial school. Emotions are either all for or all against. It is ideas that are reasoned, and consequently less interesting. The romantic, concerned with feelings, will go to a far extreme to save them, even the extreme of giving up his individuality.

American literature contains more than a few examples—Hawthorne's utopian stories, much of early Mark Twain—suggesting that he who joins the common herd is no traitor to the romantic cause. The reason is that the sensitive individual finds a new identity in his new group. Twain's innocents abroad, for example, find themselves bound together in their new identity. Their smugness and intolerance are the result of their apprehension of this new entity.

Anyone with out-of-the-ordinary intellectual or social pretensions—and the two are often equated in American films and novels—occasionally considers descending to the happy common level. He, more precisely, feels like it. No one forces Beulah Bondi to do the Big Apple. She suddenly feels like it. If you just feel like doing something you are in the happy position of not having to think about why.

It feels good to join. Spencer Tracy in *Woman of*

the Year discovers it allows him to be very smug about the fact that he can speak only English while the others at Katharine Hepburn's party speak outlandish foreign tongues. Cary Grant in *Talk of the Town* may not know legal history, but he knows American life. The normal healthy vulgarity of Ginger Rogers in *Vivacious Lady* is just the thing to cure bookish and intellectual James Stewart. All belong to something larger than themselves, all are people who have found a new and collective identity.

If it is good to join, then the person who makes others join is especially good. The proselytizer for mediocrity is a favorite figure in American pictures, and Stevens offers several variations on the theme of the mediocre man who makes others make good.

In *A Damsel in Distress*, Fred Astaire is an American innocent abroad. In love with aristocratic Joan Fontaine, he refuses to be intimidated by her nobility. Undismayed by her patrician ways, he will show her the joys of the plebian majority. His combination of presumed goodness and boundless optimism wins the day and shows both the lady and her family the error of their narrow if noble ways.

Later, more complex variations on this figure are George Eastman in *A Place in the Sun,* who, even though he does come from the wrong side of the tracks, still manages to win over rich Angela Vickers, for a time, at least; and Jett Rink in *Giant*, who puts one over on both the wealthier and the more sophisticated. That both of these men later find their triumphs hollow indicates how far Stevens and his audience had come since the simpler Astaire days. More subtle variations of the same motif are Shane, and Jesus Christ in *The Greatest Story Ever Told.* The former comes from the plains to the town and cleans it up; the latter comes from the wilderness into civilization and teaches it a lesson. Although these later appearances of the theme do not constitute the entire film—as they did in some of the earlier examples—they do indicate the need for compromise, the need of the romantic individual to find a way out of his dilemma.

"I have a great regard for your judgment in practical matters. I find it equal if not superior to my own."
"Thank you, sir."
—The Talk of the Town

This exchange between Ronald Colman, soon to become a member of the Supreme Court, and his faithful black valet, Rex Ingram, follows the scene in which Colman cuts off his beard to the accompaniment of Wagner. That sequence had concluded with a very long-held shot of Ingram looking at his master, eyes welling with tears, a single drop finally coursing its way down his faithful black cheek.

Stevens may have thought he had found a way out for the individual in suggesting that joining a group would solve his problem. That it did nothing of the sort is shown by his attitude toward those individuals who were denied the possibility of such a choice because they were stigmatized, and consequently forced to remain loners whether they wanted to or not, in a world that for them was certainly far from perfect.

The Norwegians in San Francisco in *I Remember Mama,* the Jews in Nazi-dominated Holland in *The Diary of Anne Frank*—these were minorities, stigmatized, less or more, but to both groups Stevens could extend the protection of group identification. Other stigmatized individuals, mainly Negroes, were not offered this protection, neither in Stevens' films nor in any other American films before World War II. Yet they were just as definitely individuals and, as we have now discovered, very romantic individuals indeed, being much concerned with a better world than the one they are forced to inhabit.

Sensitive to the slights experienced by Katharine Hepburn in *Alice Adams*, the director appears blind to the equally apparent misery of Hattie McDaniel as, her maid's cap wilting, she serves hot soup and sweetbreads on toast on a scorching day. Much is made of the difficulties of circus life for the white principals in *Annie Oakley*, but the equally real difficulties of the colored help in the kitchen are laughed at. We are meant to take the sorrows of Beulah Bondi and Ginger Rogers, at the end of *Vivacious Lady*, more or less seriously, but when Willie Best, the colored porter, adds a few tears of his own at the sight of white folks in distress, we are supposed to find it amusing.

Such, of course, were the conventions of commercial film during the times these pictures were made. Indeed a part of the need for this forced and always artificial laughter might have been an unacknowledged uneasiness at the treatment allocated the blacks. Such, surely, might have been Stevens' own feelings—which he acknowledged, in however empty a manner, by casting Sidney Poitier as the kind Simon of Cyrene who helps Jesus during His torments, and by the sudden, impassioned, and unconvincing plea for mixed marriages with which *Giant* ends. In any event, we need not con-

Anne Shoemaker, Fred MacMurray, Hattie McDaniel, Katharine Hepburn and Fred Stone in *Alice Adams*

gratulate ourselves upon our recently acquired hind-sight with regard to Negroes; what Stevens was doing was no different, and certainly no worse, than what anyone else during this period was doing.

If, however, he was suggesting joyful joining as a way out of the romantic dilemma, he was not doing very well. He was suggesting that only certain of the whites, attractive ones, were allowed to join. This was no answer to a problem of such philosophical impor-tance as the one he had chosen, knowingly or not, to impose upon himself.

The fact is that joining a collective identity, be it country, club, or marriage partnership, solves none of the individual's problems. These continue unchanged. And, in addition, the amount of romanticism necessary to sustain belief in this presumed escape from the romantic dilemma eventually becomes untenable for even the most romantic.

Take, for example, *Gunga Din*. Here Sam Jaffe—also colored, an Indian—is a lowly water carrier who has the ambition of becoming a real British soldier. He loses his life aborting an Indian attack so that the British army will be saved. A grand military funeral is held, during which he is posthumously made corporal. A poem is read—"You're a better man than I am, Gunga Din. . . ." Cary Grant looks sorrowful; Victor MacLaglen sniffles; Douglas Fairbanks, Jr., permits himself a near tear. Eventually the ghost of Gunga Din himself looms large over the landscape—a device to which Stevens resorts when all else fails: a monster Christ towers King-Kong-like over His disciples at the end of *The Greatest Story Ever Told*.

Somehow, it rings hollow. There are a number of

reasons why: the hypocrisy of it, the cant of it all. But, specifically, we see that joining, even if it were not done posthumously, would not solve Gunga Din's problems. They are his, they are interior, they demand more of him than a simple changing of his position in the world. Nor would joining, even if finally allowed, solve the problems of the Rex Ingrams and Hattie McDaniels. Nor, finally, will it really solve any problems for Katharine Hepburn, James Stewart, Ronald Colman, or any of the other joiners in these Stevens pictures. The problem of the individual is larger than this; it demands a larger solution.

Such a solution is indicated in *Shane, A Place in the Sun, Giant,* where the problem of the feeling individual in a society indifferent to his hopes is examined with candor and probity. For this solution to come about, however, an obstacle had to be removed, one which we are now forced to examine—sentimentality.

"You're just a normal human being leading a normal human life."
"That sounds just fine."
—Woman of the Year

Spencer Tracy has answered Fay Bainter's observation. He is a joiner, congratulates himself on his membership, sees nothing to change either in himself or in the world. In *Shane,* Alan Ladd sees much that is wrong. Feeling it is too late to do much about himself, he does his bit to make a better world, though it only means killing Jack Palance. In *Woman of the Year,* however, Tracy sees no necessity of changing. At the same time, however, he certainly feels sorry for people like the poor little Greek orphan boy whom busy Katharine Hepburn adopts and then neglects. He feels sorry, but, at the end of the picture, after Hepburn has been brought to heel, there is no further mention of the poor little Greek orphan. He seems to have been forgotten —by them, and apparently by Stevens; we, too, have presumably forgotten about him.

This is sentimentality, and Spencer Tracy is its spokesman. He, and we, enjoy feelings for which he makes himself in no way responsible. An easy tear, a chuckle or two, the reassurance that, well, life's like that. If such emotions are not followed by appropriate actions, one is left in the position of enjoying emotions without having to pay for them. For decades, producers have found this position lucrative; it is only recently that filmgoers have found it untenable.

Stevens himself has been a ruthless sentimentalist. The poor little Greek boy appears not because he is poor and little but because he provides an excuse for Spence and Kate's getting together again. In *Vigil in the Night,* a whole busload is maimed and slaughtered to prevent Carole Lombard's guilty secret from getting out. In *Penny Serenade,* hundreds are destroyed in an earthquake so that Irene Dunne's miscarriage may be successfully accomplished.

Stevens' sentimentality is usually not this brutal; more often it takes the form of celebrating, of optimistically seeing, the best side of things. Not often are little Greek boys and busloads of people sacrificed. Rather, our emotional involvement is requested for the pleasures and tribulations of an immigrant family in San Francisco, for the plight of a Jewish family holed up in Amsterdam, for a trio of rough and ready regular fellows caught

Anne Shirley and Carole Lombard in *Vigil in the Night*

in a Thugee temple in the wilds of the Khyber Pass, for a misunderstood girl in the wilds of South Renford.

A feeling man, Stevens asks for an amount of emotion for these people. A fine technician, he nearly always obtains it. Often, however, the amount asked is too much. The characters are, all too often, not really worth it, and in any event, it is rarely suggested that something be done about their plight. We experience and are then told either that we can do nothing about it, or that it is going to get better anyway.

This kind of sentimentality is perhaps seen most clearly in Stevens' treatment of women, for he has rarely refused to sentimentalize them. In this, however, he is certainly not alone. Indeed, the American attitude toward women in general has long been the romantic attitude toward woman in particular. She is either the ideal, the promise of some better state toward which we aspire, or she is the anti-ideal, reminder of some worse state to which we are in danger of returning. In either case the thought does not occur that she is, after all, human, that she makes up half of mankind, that she is neither more nor less than she happens to be. This would not be a romantic thought.

Alice must either spurn local society and find happiness in her own way, or she must join this society and find happiness according to its standards. That she might compromise by going to secretarial school and working to learn something about herself and her world is not a thought that occurs to the American romantic.

Stevens' sentimentalization of women never takes the form of denigration. Just as he refused to invert his idealism and cultivate an easy cynicism, so he rejects an equally easy denigration. Rather, Barbara Stanwyck gives up her career in *Annie Oakley* because she nobly refuses to be unfeminine enough to win in a man's world; Carole Lombard in *Vigil in the Night* takes the blame for a careless sister and turns down romance that she may continue to serve as a nurse; Irene Dunne makes endless sacrifices and never gets her winter coat, in *I Remember Mama,* because she realizes that her family needs her. This kind of woman is a romantic idealization.

Or, at least, she has the possibility of being one and can learn how. Jean Arthur, career girl in *The More the Merrier,* learns how to fling away career in the interest of romance; a bit hoydenish in *Talk of the Town,* she learns how to behave like a real lady. Katharine Hepburn in *Quality Street* tries to hurry romance, but learns that it is the woman's lot to love and wait; in *Woman of the Year* she learns that woman's place is neither at the editorial desk, nor in the kitchen, but someplace in between, in Spencer Tracy's arms; Irene Dunne learns in *Penny Serenade* that she cannot be a true woman until she is also a mother; Ginger Rogers in *Vivacious Lady* learns that she cannot be a true woman until she is also a wife; and Dorothy McGuire, as the Virgin Mary, learns that she is not to be allowed womanhood at all—she must remain the mute, appealing, personified ideal.

Women are pure, or capable of purity; selfless, or capable of selflessness. They are a breed apart, a cut above. The sentimentality of this concept lies in the assumption that women have so nearly attained an ideal and perfect state that nothing remains but to keep them in it. The fact that nothing else in this world exhibits such a propensity toward perfection does not disturb the romantic. Woman is the beacon of hope, the ray of light in the darkness. This established, nothing need be done to face the problems of real women in the real world.

It will be noticed in such idealizations as these that it is the men who indicate to women their ideal state, or else indicate how such a state may be achieved. In *Woman of the Year,* Katharine Hepburn has lost her femininity. She does not know how to make her man his breakfast. One of Stevens' longest comedy sequences shows the mess she consequently makes. In *Penny Serenade,* Irene Dunne, in very unfeminine fashion, does not know how to bathe the baby. In one of the longest takes he ever filmed, Stevens lovingly shows her hesitation, indecision, inability.

And in both instances it is the man who steps in, offers solutions to the problems. Now that they have learned, these two chastened women will be able to make breakfasts and bathe babies with the best. They will become ideal, but it is men who showed them how.

Since this is male propaganda, we are not to believe that women give up anything in particular to better bathe babies. It would not occur to the romantic male, so much in need of an ideal in this imperfect world, to consider that: Katharine Hepburn was much more herself as a columnist; Irene Dunne was more satisfied selling phonograph records; Ginger Rogers was better suited to be a dance instructor; Joan Fontaine was happier as an English lady of leisure—all positions from which men rescued them that they might reach the heights of an ideal womanhood. The fact that, in real life as well as screen life, hundreds of women daily exchange a salient part of themselves for some man's

Cary Grant and Irene Dunne in *Penny Serenade*

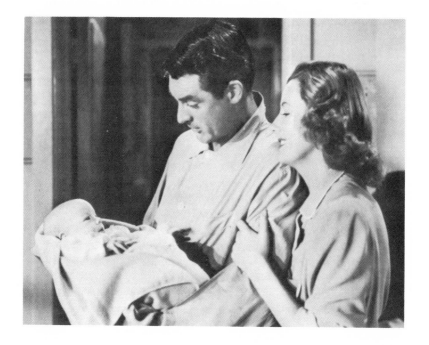

romantic ideal does not indicate that the romantic image of women has any validity. It demonstrates the power of the woman's biology and the man's brainwashing.

Not, however, that Stevens was incapable of creating real women on the screen, unidealized, unromanticized —Elizabeth Taylor in *Giant,* Shelley Winters in *A Place in the Sun,* Jean Arthur in *Shane,* even Millie Perkins in *The Diary of Anne Frank*—these are real women and their imperfections are faithfully observed. Until World War II, however, Stevens remained a full romantic, one of Hollywood's finest examples.

To recapitulate, Stevens' idealization and consequent sentimentalization of women was predicated both upon a need to give some indication of a better world than this one, and upon a hope, however impractical, that the mere display of such an ideal personified would perhaps effect some change. This in turn was based upon romantic optimism, the belief that somehow the change would come. This belief rested upon a strong conviction of the innate good in all men. And this, finally, was founded on the basic assumption that good, like faith, springs from feeling rather than thought, and that it is therefore the subjective emotions which are to be trusted in life.

"Stop crying—you're spoiling the invasion."
—The Diary of Anne Frank

Stevens as a romantic was very much a product of his times, and his films continued to reinforce romantic ideals. Perhaps this is one of the reasons Stevens has always been a popular director. Before the war, you could go to see almost any of his films knowing that

Katharine Hepburn in *Woman of the Year*

Spencer Tracy and Katharine Hepburn in *Woman of the Year*

the director's assumptions were your own.

Stevens himself felt that this was as it should be. He worked both with and for his audience. Once he told Herbert Luft: "The audience is my boss. If people who go to see films continue to like my work I can stay in the business that I love. If they don't, which I hope will never happen, I'll have to find something else to do."

He was a director who paid attention to what the public liked and gave it to them. To read his filmography is consequently like reading a history of popular movie taste during the thirties and forties: sentimental romances, followed by screwball comedies, followed by social-interest melodramas—an accurate reflection of the changing tastes of the movie public.

What the public wanted was what he wanted to give. If possible he held previews of his new films and changed the picture according to audience reaction, taking out a scene that didn't seem to work, putting in one that hopefully would. Like many directors of his period—in particular, directors of comedy, his original field—he always wanted to test his work before he released it. Unlike many, however, he wanted to get the audience reaction even if the picture was not a comedy. And, unlike the majority, he was not cynical; he trusted his audience and really wanted to please it.

His excesses may almost all be ascribed to this willingness, even this need, to please his audience. Having learned, for example, from early days that easy laughs are always welcome, he studded his films with them. James Ellison and Ginger Rogers get into a taxi. They stumble and fall in. There is no reason why they should except that it is an easy laugh. Some suitcases are lying around. Fred Astaire turns to go. He trips over them. Another easy laugh. Charles Coburn regards the Big Apple with astonishment. His monocle falls not once, but twice. Another easy laugh. To remember these films is to remember the ubiquitous Eric Blore. If all his double takes, as they occur in Stevens' pictures, were spliced end to end, they might, one feels, make a feature in themselves.

An easy laugh, an easy tear, these are the things that an audience likes, or, at least, that the audience of that period liked. George Stevens, a sentimental romantic, made films for a nation of sentimental romantics.

At the same time, however, he was doing more than this. He was creating a style, perfecting an already well-grounded technical assurance, and readying himself for the post-romantic films he made after the war, which were to prove his finest.

Unlike many American directors, Stevens had first come to the movies by way of the camera. He knew how it worked and what it was capable of. He saw film not through the typewriter but through the camera's finder. This was no unmixed advantage; it led him, for example, to tolerate grave weaknesses in his scripts, but it assured his early familiarity with what movies are about—a machine that takes pictures.

Getting a scene on film in the best way, however, sometimes ranked higher than writing the scene so that it would play in the best way, or editing the scene so that it would show in the best way. Stevens closest involvement seemed to be with the cameraman and the actors rather than with the writer or the editor.

This led him into miscalculations which marred many of his pictures. His confidence in improvisation, gained in filming the early comedies, and often, the pressure of a schedule allowed him to begin pictures which had not been completely written. *Annie Oakley* was begun with only a third of the script prepared; the rest was somehow figured out. The script for *Swing Time* was redone completely just before shooting and was finished during filming. The all-laughing finale of this picture, like the all-crying finale of *Vivacious Lady,* another film with an unfinished script, was put together on the spur of the last moment. *Gunga Din* was begun with a continuity only two-thirds written, and some scenes— the one between Cary Grant and Sam Jaffe about the bugle, for example—were improvised on the spot. Only two-thirds of *Woman of the Year* was done when the picture was begun. The final kitchen scene was decided upon only during the last days of shooting. And so on.

This was, to be sure, nothing extraordinary. It was common practice in the film-factory days. The producers had their deadlines and their budget problems as well as their commitments to the distributors. They did not care what went on the screen as long as something did. Stevens' actions ought to be explained, however, because he proved himself more important than the rest of the film-factory employees. He had the power to assert his directorial rights, and could refuse to budge until he had a script of which he approved. If he was not allowed these rights he had the option of quitting.

Yet he, who has always preferred a finished script, who likes to film with the greatest care, who is fond of long rehearsals, etc., did nothing of the sort. In this he was sustained by his experience and the optimistic belief that things would somehow or other turn out all right. This romantic notion may have salved his conscience and satisfied his producers, but it was incompatible with the director Stevens became. The all-laughing or all-crying finale cannot succeed as resolution even to musical comedy or screwball farce; that bugle scene is amateurish and unbelievable; the kitchen scene solves none of the problems to which the audience has been led to expect resolutions.

Perhaps Stevens was subscribing to the notion, very much with us nowadays, that a spontaneous scene shot off the cuff is somehow more authentic than a finished one which came from the mind of a writer. Such a scene is now thought to reek of reality. If the camera shakes or the focus is off, there is presumably greater actuality. These assumptions are romantic to the core and suggest a kind of inchoate innocence both behind the camera and in front of it—that the feelings expressed by a person who is not acting and a cameraman who is not pulling his focus properly are of much greater interest than the ideas of either of them. Such methods succeed—and they often do—only if the scene successfully conveys this innocence, and if the context of the film as a whole has prepared you for it.

Stevens obviously never went this far. He always exercised control, but often he did not exercise enough, either over the picture or himself. Yet, at the same time, his almost exclusive concern for the scene and what went on in front of the camera led very early to the formation of an extraordinary talent for handling actors and a corresponding respect for their efforts. Katharine Hepburn, Ginger Rogers, Charles Coburn, Irene Dunne, Beulah Bondi, Jean Arthur, Oscar Homolka, Montgomery Clift, Shelley Winters, Alan Ladd, Elizabeth Taylor— all of these were at their best under Stevens' direction.

He sometimes created their excellences, sometimes observed them. In *Alice Adams* the camera sits back, as it were, and records what is happening; at other times there are dozens of created felicities: Charles Coburn saying hello to his alarm clock; Jean Arthur, knees buckling, during a love scene; Moroni Olsen as Buffalo Bill lovingly doing up his long hair; Estelle Winwood being delicately arch about someone else's love life; Cary Grant and Irene Dunne, drawn to each other, trying to go out the door at the same time; the acutely observed detail in the ensemble acting in *I Remember Mama* and *The Diary of Anne Frank*.

A movie director, willy-nilly or purposely, chooses his themes; at the same time, and in the same way, he decides how he will show or illustrate these themes. Stevens may be defined through the themes he chose and the stories he filmed. He chose, however, from what was available to him, and his image as a romantic evolved partially from himself as a person, and partially from the romantic nature of the audience he was making films for and the romantic repertoire they were presumably insisting upon. He may be further defined by the way he told his story and showed his theme, again, remembering that his choice was limited by the conventions of the American motion picture industry at the time. Stevens' style was one, as we shall see, in which form and content were unified, or nearly unified most of the time. It was also one which was limited, defined, and sustained by the conventions under which he worked.

Stevens constructed most of his earlier films according to accepted pattern. Statement, exposition, development, climax—these are the standard units of the standard

Charles Coburn in *The More the Merrier*

film, and even now his structure, though much more personal, adheres to this formula. Having had experience as a cameraman and assistant director, Stevens knew from the first about these standard units. Later he learned how to make them flow one into the other. Still later he learned how to change them—how to break the rules.

In his earliest pictures, however, one sees preferences or predilections which run throughout his work. One of these is a fondness for reaction. Given the choice Stevens will choose to show the effect that something makes rather than the thing itself. At its most primitive the effect is Eric Blore doing yet another double take. At its most sophisticated, as in *Shane*, it results in a heightened atmosphere of confrontation, one reaction setting off another. Used exclusively, however, it can also mitigate.

In *The Greatest Story Ever Told*, for example, Jesus raises Lazarus. The camera backs farther and farther away. When the miracle finally occurs we are so far away we can see nothing. We are shown, instead, shot after shot of the reactions of those who are watching this surprising event. Sensing that this is not enough for a happening of this importance, Stevens then sends Sal Mineo and Ed Wynn running to the city to give the happy news. There is shot after shot of their running, stumbling, running again. Giving news of the event has become more important than the event itself, just as seeing its effect was considered more important than seeing it.

Compare this, then, with the miracle in *Ordet*. Dreyer makes us watch it. We see it with our own eyes. And we believe. No amount of furious running, furious cutting, will create in an audience the amount of emotion Stevens sacrificed in deliberately choosing to shoot his scene in this fashion.

Yet, it is typical that he would so choose. Believing in emotions, he is eager to show these emotions. To a romantic the intensity of emotion generated is always more important than whatever it is that generates the emotion. To show Sal Mineo looking astonished and Ed Wynn moving blind eyes to heaven is, so Stevens thought—or better, felt—a way of making us all feel the emotionality of the situation. Only, as we have seen, it isn't.

But then, at moments of great emotion, the Stevens camera does tend not to look, or, at least, to back away. After the accidental drowning in *A Place in the Sun,* for example, the camera is suddenly far from the action. The hero reaches the shore in the far, far distance.

Not that Stevens has no use for big close-ups. His later use of enormous close shots has become one of the identifying marks of his style. His way of using them, however, indicates the continuing romantic nature of his ideas.

In *Giant* we see the self-destructive sister on a bucking horse. There is a sudden cut, an enormous close-up of her spur digging into the animal's flank. Then there is a long, slow shot of the horse returning riderless.

In *A Place in the Sun* we are given an enormous close-up of Alice—almost her first in the entire film— just before the moment, not shown, when she drowns. After the flurry in the water we see, from a long distance, George Eastman emerging from the lake alone.

These close-ups are used to make an emotional impact before the emotion-arousing event (death by falling from a horse, death by drowning), and the results of the event are shown in long shot. The effect is that of making us emotionally involved before the fact. After the fact we are deliberately disinvolved. This is elegiac. We experience the emotion but not its consequences. We are not shown either lady dead, for example. Instead, an aesthetic appeal is instantly made. Those beautiful shots of horse wandering off, boy emerging from lake, suggest by both their nature and their context that emotion to be experienced is suddenly over. We are invited to contemplate, to feel, and at the same time to refrain from action. These are reaction shots in which the audience's reactions to something, death in this case, are more important than the action itself. In neither case do we view the death; the instant elegy that follows is what the romantic poets would have called a dying fall. The final shot softens rather than heightens the impact of the shots preceding.

Another softening device much used by Stevens is the dissolve. He does not use this punctuation in the orthodox Hollywood way. Rather, he has made it, like the close-up, personal, even idiosyncratic. Sometimes its use is very creative and completely effective.

In *A Place in the Sun* there is a beautiful example. George Eastman is looking at the lake. There is a slow dissolve to Alice Tripp waiting for him. The dissolve is so slow that Alice appears to be in the lake, which is just where she will eventually end. There is a double dissolve in the same film that works admirably. Eastman and Angela are dancing, and there is a slow dissolve to the solitary bedroom where Alice is waiting for him. At the same time, and just as slowly, the ballroom waltz, lush, full of romantic promise, dissolves to that

most tawdry of sounds, the electric organ music of a
late radio program.

Also in this picture is a complicated and satisfying
multiple dissolve. Alice's death is being reported over
the radio. This news, however, is shortly submerged by
the sound of a motor boat, a noise associated with the
wealthy Angela. At the same time we hear the haunting
call of the loon, a cry used to unspecified and perhaps
consequently haunting effect in the picture. In the mean-
time the camera has been looking at Angela's summer
residence, the place where Eastman had come closest
to what he wanted. Now it is boarded up, summer is
over, life has gone. These associations created, we
suddenly hear the sound of the judge's gavel, and it
becomes apparent that this short but elaborate sequence
is really a bridge, introducing the court scenes. The loon
is heard for the final time, raising its individual and
solitary voice. The gavel raps, drowning it out, the
noise of society itself.

The dissolve—in painting, in music, in films—is a
purposeful blurring of line or image. Its effect is the
opposite of severely juxtaposed areas in painting, the
formal presentation of one theme after another in
music, the simple cut in film. All of these suggest that
there is a sequential order, that one thing is separate
from another, that a usual sequence of events is to be
expected in the world as it is. The implications are
realistic—this is the way things are and the way they
therefore should be represented. The dissolve implies
the opposite. It suggests connections that are subjective,
prophetic, elegiac, or magical.

Somewhat like the magical connections of Stevens'
dissolves are those contrasts, seemingly fortuitous, which

account for much of the best in his films. In *Penny Serenade* it is New Year's Eve, and Cary Grant has just asked Irene Dunne if she won't marry him and eventually go off to Tokyo. They kiss. At that instant it is suddenly the new year. Bells, snow, whistles, shouts —and a private celebration is suddenly public, magically augmented. In *The Diary of Anne Frank,* Millie Perkins and Richard Beymer finally kiss. At that moment we hear the screech of a police car stopping outside. Again, it is magic, though in this case black magic.

Such sudden contrasts, all of them giving a shock which heightens emotion, abound in Stevens' pictures. Sometimes they are playful. In *Swing Time* Ginger Rogers hears Fred Astaire singing and playing the piano. Forgetting that she is in the middle of washing her hair and consequently all sudsy, she wanders into the room, and he turns, surprised, for he has been serenading her with the flattering and romantic "The Way You Look Tonight." In *The More the Merrier* there is a similar scene where the neat, punctual, very efficient Jean Arthur is suddenly revealed sloppy, with cream on her face and a toothbrush in her mouth. Another playful contrast in the same picture occurs when the lovers switch on the light in the hall of the crowded apartment and discover that it is full of bedding-down people who could find no place to sleep in crowded wartime Washington, and that their supposed solitary love-making has, in fact, been in company. Almost the same scene occurs in *Vivacious Lady,* where James Stewart and Ginger Rogers, hoping to be alone, wander into the boathouse. Upon turning on the light they discover that the boathouse is full of people doing just

Ginger Rogers and James Stewart in *Vivacious Lady*

Joel McCrea and Jean Arthur in *The More the Merrier*

what they had hoped to do.

Sometimes, however, the contrasts serve as portent. In *Giant*, James Dean, having just discovered oil on his property, runs to tell the rich folks. He runs to the front porch and leans against one of the white pillars. When he has departed we see that he has left a black, oiled handprint on the pillars. The black and white contrast is here presumed to symbolize one of the themes of the film.

The nicest of these many contrasts are those that do not have to work so hard, that exist merely for their own sakes. In *Annie Oakley* there has been a great deal of activity about the sharpshooting contest. Suddenly, there is a scene in which the whole cast is present, but no one is moving. It is a still picture and the contrast is enormous. Then it is revealed that it is truly a still picture. They are having their picture taken and must not move during the process. One of the best occurs in one of the lesser pictures, *Quality Street*. Katharine Hepburn has been impersonating her fictitious niece. She is now off to a dance, or something. In the next room the others are talking about her. One of them asks if the other remembers what Aunt Kate was like when she was younger. At that instant the door opens and there stands Hepburn looking just as she had ten years before. It is a magical moment.

The implications of such contrasts, like the implications of the dissolve, rest upon the assumption of an ideal world in which such rightness could occur, rare though it is in the world we know. Again, it is the world as it ought to be and so rarely is.

Another romantic attribute of Stevens' style is the visual expression of a theme that occurs, perhaps unplanned, in his earliest films and is of paramount importance in his later work. The theme is his personal concept of the outsider, the loser—the icon for its illustration is the window.

Windows are proportionately more common in the movies than they are in life. Movies are about seeing, about looking into, about a kind of voyeurism, if you like, and are so used by many directors—Hitchcock, for example. No one but Stevens, however, uses windows in so peculiar and personal a fashion.

Alice Adams comes back from the dance. Unhappy, she goes to her room, walks to the window, bursts into tears. The camera is moved outside; we see the window, rain beating against it, tears flowing behind it. In *Quality Street* the windows become so many eyes, with the camera staring out or peeping in. In *Vigil in the Night,* the camera first discovers Carole Lombard behind a window. Later, when she breaks down and cries, the camera retreats again, outside the window. In *Talk of the Town,* when Jean Arthur and Ronald Colman finally meet again, the camera moves outside the window and peers in. *The More the Merrier* makes much use of windows, the camera usually peering into the rooms. In *Shane,* the principals are always seen looking out of the windows. *I Remember Mama* is full of window shots —it even has one in the credits.

The thing about a window is that someone is on the inside of it and someone is on the outside. Stevens uses this several ways, but usually he puts the spectator outside. This means that the viewer is the outsider. He is purposely cut off from the compelling situation (Hepburn or Lombard in tears), for, just as Stevens backs away from the big climax and its consequences, so he puts this pane of glass in front of the emotional consequences of a situation.

The theme common to the majority of Stevens' pictures is that of the outsider; the story of these pictures is how the outsider reacts to his situation. Stevens' unique use of windows reinforces this theme by insisting that the viewer become an outsider, even to the point of being consequently less moved by the emotions which Stevens is, at the same time, taking all of this trouble to show him. The attitude of the director is ambivalent, and so remained until he redefined the role of the outsider in his later films, until he himself became artist enough to realize what his pictures were really about.

The theme of the outsider is visually conveyed in other ways, among them the manner in which Stevens groups and composes his scenes. Alice Adams is at the party which will later make her so unhappy. All the dancers, mainly in black evening clothes, flock to the dance floor. Alice, all in contrasting white, is left alone up in one corner of the screen, not knowing what to do with herself. The composition shows the situation.

Again, in the "Fine Romance" number from *Swing Time,* Fred Astaire and Ginger Rogers are mad at each other. Hence Stevens separates them, putting each at a corner of the screen. These are fairly simple examples. *Shane* and *Giant* offer more complicated groupings. In the banquet scene in the latter picture, the three themes of the film—the great family and its powerful heritage, the son who defies it, the outsider who takes advantage of it—all come together, the composition of these elements explaining the collisions of these three ideas.

Often Stevens creates a physical setting which reflects his themes. One remembers the dinner tables of

Gunga Din

Alice Adams and *I Remember Mama,* or the front porches of the houses. Sometimes the geography itself helps to illustrate the theme, becomes a symbol. The story of *Shane* remains in the memory as a flat valley backed by high mountains, with a one-street town and a cemetery; *Gunga Din* is a solitary temple set high in the Khyber Pass; *Giant* is an American Gothic mansion set flat on the Texas plains.

All of these memorable images share an isolation— physical, social, economic. They mirror the qualities of being different, being alone, being individual. They reflect the continuing theme—the outsider, the solitary, the individual alone. And they indicate without insisting. In order for Stevens to have been able to create such images it was necessary for him to have matured, to have found a way out of the romantic dilemma. And he did.

"All you can do is raise them. You can't live their lives for them."
—*Giant*

The final escape from the romantic dilemma, the ultimate solution to the problem of self versus society, lies in the determination to be an artist, in attitude if not in deed—to make somehow visible the interior struggle, to project the problem into a work of art, even if the work of art is one's own life.

Stevens, master craftsman turned artist, made this decision. He made it late, but then making it at all assumes maturation. The reason that so many Americans never do is that our society has had little experience; it was founded upon romantic premises, and perhaps

Steve Brown, Peggy McIntyre, June Hedin, Barbara Bel Geddes and Irene Dunne in *I Remember Mama*

consequently the youthful and romantic virtues are those openly insisted upon. Maturity is unpopular. This would suggest that romanticism itself, certainly in America, is a product of spiritual adolescence, and such it seems to be.

Several reasons have been brought forward for Stevens' postwar change. Among them has been the fact that society itself changed to an almost unrecognizable extent; another makes much of his war experiences, so harrowing that optimistic sentimentality was largely banished from his thoughts and his works. And these reasons are valid, but certainly equally important is that Stevens, a late bloomer like so many Americans, was ready after the war to mature in the way of which, we now see, he was capable.

It is this which makes Stevens—quite beyond the excellences of many of his films—an extremely interesting director. He is very much a part of something larger than himself. Standing almost as the epitome of his place and time, he also reveals in his artistic evolution possibilities concerning his country and its future.

As Stevens himself became an artist his attitude changed. Katrin in *I Remember Mama* has written this novel about her family. Whatever her thoughts, her feelings, whatever their contradictions, she has both resolved and objectified them in a book. She has projected her personal problems into a work of art.

The difference in attitude in this later film is noticeable if one compares it with that in *Penny Serenade*. The heroine in the latter aimlessly plays old phonograph records and passively enjoys her bittersweet memories. Since she does nothing further, hers is a sentimental reverie, pleasant enough in itself, but meaningless. Katrin has done something more with her own ambivalent memories. She has created from them, has ordered her past, and, to that extent, has changed it. Like Anne Frank, she defines herself through this redefinition of herself. She becomes—and the word is the antithesis of romantic—objective.

She is also largely unbelievable, and her picture of her life is largely sentimental in its making so much of things not worth making that much over. But a new attitude is present. Objective, analytical, she—and, one feels, Stevens himself—is freed from the limitations of simply subjectively feeling one's life. Rather, she is objectively thinking about it. She is Alice Adams grown up.

The objective attitude, quite different from the subjective, is to try to see the world as it is. That it is as it is, is enough; one need not hope for one somehow different. This attitude is not, therefore, concerned with celebrating the world, nor with denigrating it. Both of these are romantic attitudes. Rather, it is concerned with living in the world, with finding out what it is really like, with interpreting it. This is the attitude of the mature artist. The way out of the romantic dilemma is to turn from romanticism.

A Place in the Sun indicates the process. George Eastman, sympathetic, ambitious, sees the world more or less as it is, and wants his share of its good things. A wealthy girl, Angela, comes to symbolize for him all of those good things. At the same time he has Alice, a poor girl. Her pregnancy gets in the way of his love affair with Angela. Unable to see any other solution, he begins to feel about this, allows himself to play with the idea of murder. Accidentally, she does get killed. Almost as accidentally, he is convicted of murder.

The differences between the assumptions of this film and of, say, *Alice Adams*, are apparent. The social schism is there, but it is not the real problem. Stevens has already gone beyond that. The problem lies within George Eastman himself, just as the real problem, and its solution, lay within Alice Adams herself. The difference is that *A Place in the Sun* shows us this.

Self-knowledge is the solution to the problem. Shane, Jesus Christ, know this. George Eastman knows more than Alice Adams, but he does not know that much.

He knows himself up to a point, quite unlike the hero of the Dreiser novel upon which the film is based, who is a symbol of confusion, a pawn of fate. Sensitive, both to himself and to the outside world, he is not portrayed within the simple dichotomy of the romantic view. Not in store for him the spurious comforts of a magical happy ending or a sudden joining of something larger than himself. He cannot escape the consequences of being who he is.

At the beginning of the picture, Eastman is hitch-hiking. He is standing in front of a billboard—a girl on a beach, the personification of all that George wants. A roadster races by. Driving it is Angela, the girl he will eventually love. As he looks after her, he hears a horn. It is a broken-down truck, stopping to give him a lift. Alice Adams would have refused to get in. George Eastman does no such thing. He does not wait for another roadster to, perhaps, stop. He gets in.

Eventually, however, he falters. He has defined himself up to a point, but there comes a further point when he forgets that emotions are, after all, only ideas. He begins to believe in what he feels. Feeling himself caught in the situation with the pregnant Alice, he loses his

Montgomery Clift in *A Place in the Sun*

objectivity, begins to toy with the idea of murder and other impractical ways out.

Stevens shows us this, but he does not agree with it—not the way that he agreed with Fred Astaire's making it in the big town or Katharine Hepburn's giving up herself for her man. His film was, after all, based on *An American Tragedy,* and Stevens had discovered what that tragedy was and is.

The typical American tragedy is the typical romantic tragedy. Alone and in a world he never made, the individual is driven—say the romantics—to emotional excesses that result in murder or suicide. There are various ways of explaining this—Dreiser's, for example, was that the hero is the way he is because his society made him that way.

Stevens apparently, however, could no longer believe anything as simplistic as this. For him a man had become what he does, and must take full and personal responsibility for both his heredity and his early environment. It is not what was done to you that matters; it is what you do with what was done to you.

The climax of the film takes place in the courtroom. It is not the first time that Stevens had brought his climax to court—there were the interrupted trial in *Talk of the Town,* the child-welfare hearings in *Penny Serenade,* the investigation in *Vigil in the Night,* and there would be the trial in *The Greatest Story Ever Told*—but it was the first time that the accused was not acquitted. Before, the innocent remained always innocent; now, the innocent are guilty.

This is tragic. You do your best with what has been done to you, and still you are condemned. The reasons for Eastman's being sentenced have little to do with

Shelley Winters and Montgomery Clift in *A Place in the Sun*

Elizabeth Taylor and Montgomery Clift in *A Place in the Sun*

Eastman himself. Although, as Eugene Archer has noted, Stevens does not quite dare "end the film on a note of social criticism by implying that a man whose plan for murder resulted in a girl's death could be both legally and morally innocent," the intentions of the director are quite clear.

It was the first time that Stevens had openly criticized society. He did not criticize Eastman, understanding him far too well for that. Rather, and rightly, he criticized society for criticizing him, for its insensitivity, for its values that created his dilemma. The differences in attitude between this film and the ones which went before are extreme, as are the implications of these differences.

In *A Place in the Sun* and films that followed, one sees these implications. There is no better world; this is the only one there is. If you cannot live in it as it is, then fight it. The world may be to blame, but simply blaming it doesn't help. Be brave enough to admit who you are. You are an outsider, a loner, and, if necessary, a renegade. The way to escape from the romantic dilemma, this pain of being an outsider, is to admit just that—that one is an outsider. If you admit that you are outside and that you are just as much a part of this world in being so, then you need not search for a way to escape, for you have already escaped. You are ready to fight the world, to change it. The way you have discovered you can do this is through a knowledge of yourself.

In *Shane,* toward the middle of the picture the hero is talking to the leader of the cattlemen. "Your days are over," says Shane. "Mine? What about yours, gunslinger?" asks the cattleman. "The difference is, I know

Montgomery Clift (left) and Raymond Burr (standing, right) in
A Place in the Sun

it," answers Shane. And he is right. That is the major difference, the only one that makes any difference.

Shane sees the world as it is precisely because he is an outsider. He came from nowhere and he is going nowhere—like the vagrant Jett Rink in *Giant*, like the hitchhiking George Eastman, like Jesus Christ. It is because he is going nowhere and because he is so outside that he can see clearly, objectively. His difference from the romantic hero is that he—like Christ himself—rather than merely feeling that he ought do something to express his inner values and to affect the world, actually does something about it. As James Silke has observed, the characteristic Stevens' theme, from the first, has certainly been that of the individual trying to live in a society that does not want him. Now, however, this individual has become a man of action. He will no longer attempt to change himself. Rather, he will try to change the world. Stevens, however, does not show us this directly.

Shane opens with Alan Ladd descending into the valley in which he will spend the remainder of the picture. This action is viewed behind the credits. The opening sequence, however, is not about Alan, but about a little boy, Brandon de Wilde, who is playing at shooting deer near the cabin where he lives with his father and mother. It is he who looks up and sees Shane. It is he whom we watch watching at the end of the picture. Thus, from the first, we do not see Shane so much through our eyes as through the eyes of a child.

The romantic, with his strong interest in things as they ought to be rather than things as they are, has an especial fondness for the child or adult, who, in the face of corroding experience, manages to cling to his

Alan Ladd and Brandon de Wilde in *Shane*

John Dierkes, Emile Meyer and Jack Palance in *Shane*

innocence. The child is the most agreeable symbol for this quality, because, according to the romantic imagination, the child is innately good. To be sure, everyone is, but the child is somehow more so since he has not yet been dirtied by life, has not had to compromise this ideal. That Stevens never made much of children earlier in his career is somewhat surprising. The child would have made an eloquent spokesman for the romantic attitude. One might, indeed, imagine a *Shane* made around, say, 1935, in which the youngster would have played an even larger part.

It would have begun much in the same way as the 1953 film, but instead of Alan Ladd's slow and convincing resolve to side with Jean Arthur, Van Heflin, and the little boy, we would have had alternatives.

One of them, if we remember the convolutions Stevens went through in finding a way out of the dilemma which he shared with the majority of his countrymen, would have been the instant happy ending. Little Brandon, eventually aided by a strong if silent Alan, would have pointed out to the cattlemen and their hired guns that shooting and killing are bad, at which they would have agreed and maybe formed a square-dance finale, with Ladd gracefully joining the mother in a quadrille, which would lightly suggest a romantic involvement, the consequences of which—adultery—we would never have to face because the end title would be coming up shortly.

Another would have the youngster machinating between farmers and cattlemen to arrange just the kind of compromise which, in the 1953 picture, Van Heflin turns down flatly. After all, why not join the cattle folks? They aren't so bad, really, just kill a few

Alan Ladd (left) in *Shane*

people now and then, and besides, cows are nice. Van, Jean, Brandon, and eventually an originally disapproving but finally won-over Shane would have joined up with the adversaries, and the film would have ended on a big barbecue scene, with the child a hero and Shane gruffly admitting that the young had something to them after all.

It would have been an either/or picture, and the romantic view would, in either, have predominated. In the *Shane* Stevens actually made, however, such was not the case. We see the hero through the romantic eyes of a child, all right, but must watch as the scales fall from those eyes. At the end of the film the child has recognized Shane's failure to justify the romantic and idealist legend he has constructed around him. "Shane, come back," is the cry of innocence in pain. The boy is calling for the return of his own pristine state, and he will never be the same.

Stevens knows what it means for a romantic to lose his romanticism. In this and other of his later films he chooses to show us the post-romantic individual through the eyes of characters themselves romantic, and then to record that painful awakening to the real world which is the lot of all of us, if we live long enough.

Anne Frank cannot initially comprehend the nature of the world in which she tragically finds herself. The film about her is about a loss of innocence that allows her finally to comprehend this nature as indifferent, quite unconcerned with right or wrong. Christ, to be sure, was either never innocent in this romantic sense, or he never lost this innocence. Unable to resolve this question, Stevens in *The Greatest Story Ever Told* substitutes the conventional romantic view. It is shared by all of

James Dean in two scenes from *Giant*

those who view Christ, and is probably why we see so much of Sal Mineo—chief romantic viewer—in the picture. He—though innocent to the last—plays the little boy to Max von Sydow's Shane.

In *Giant* we find the little boy from *Shane* grown up. He is now Jett Rink, as played by James Dean, and has remained innocent. In this film, we find that we are looking at the Benedict family not directly but, in the manner of *Shane*, through the eyes of innocence. Jett admires, emulates, even makes up romantic legends about them. Then, James Dean, just like Brandon de Wilde, discovers that his heroes are not ideal. He also discovers that he is not ideal. When he comes apart at the end of the picture, drunken, maudlin, he is the little boy from *Shane* grown old, and undone by a reality which he never really apprehended.

What happens to many of these romantics, is that knowledge comes too late. Maturity is shortly followed by death. They no longer have the energy to do anything with their new knowledge. They are merely bewildered by it.

By truthfully presenting the only sincere view, the tragic view, by continually filming an "American tragedy," Stevens suggests that there is something more, however, something further. In feeling, and showing, the tragic sense of life, he provides for a further dimension. The end may be tragic but the situation is not hopeless: one may celebrate this tragedy and yet affirm mankind.

"In spite of everything, I still believe that people are really good at heart."
—*The Diary of Anne Frank*

The romantic, in his search for a better world, notoriously rarely bothers to define this one. He may complain or fret about it, but since he does not examine it, he remains largely blind to its horror. Busy with some personal utopia, or with something as amorphous as somehow realizing the American dream, he does not feel the full impact of the world as it really is—a wilderness controlled by forces only dimly comprehended, a desert in which he, the individual, is not even so much as a grain of sand. Creature of a small civilization which has maintained a long and bitter argument with nature, he bickers, ignorant of the real world, impatient with the society which he and others have created.

When the romantic becomes so dissatisfied as to step outside his civilized world, however, he suddenly becomes aware of the nature of the world he in reality also inhabits. Leaving the hothouse, he finds himself in the jungle. His subjective feelings are of no use to him any longer; only his ability to think objectively, to see objectively—his intelligence—will save him now. The romantic who has gone beyond romanticism, who has gone so far as to recognize himself as an outsider, puts himself outside the civilized pale and quite suddenly confronts things as they really are.

Civilization is, in itself, a kind of romanticism. Outside its walls, those civilized values—the importance of intentions, the promise of the future, the degree of purpose—by which we live are rendered meaningless. A man is flatly what he does, neither less nor more. To wander outside, to know that one is an outsider, is, therefore, to realize this blank indifference to everything but action.

Shane knew this, just as Christ knew this. One may kill, the other may bring back to life—not the nature of the action is important, but the fact of action itself. Action will not occur, however, without a reason, and this is also the responsibility of the outsider. One killed and the other restored, but the reason was the same and is the only reason possible—the reason for the choice, always the same, is that it is in this way, and only in this way, that one may affirm. Shane and Christ affirm themselves by showing in action what they believe. In this they are like all heroes, and in the same way Stevens is like all artists.

The artist, faced with indifference, recognizing that he inhabits a howling wilderness, yet at the same time rejecting the spurious comforts of the collective lie that his society represents, has only the choice of giving up or going on. If he goes on—and this is what the artist does—then, despite his knowledge of his own minute place in the universe, despite his knowing his own frailty, he will—absurd as it may seem to him—affirm himself, what he believes, what he is.

One thinks of Anne Frank, one thinks of Jesus. Despite all evidence to the contrary, despite death, they chose to believe, to affirm, to say yes to life, to experience—even to their own experiences. This affirmation in the face of knowledge is an entirely different thing from the ignorant and facile affirmation of the man who has no idea of the horror that life can become.

Stevens had been such a facile optimist. That he now wanted to make a film about Christ, about Anne Frank, showed how he had changed, how he had matured. He had seen concentration camps; during the war he had experienced the full horror of a natural and indifferent world entering through the broken walls of civilization. A warm, generous man, he understood and felt a bit of the terror that Anne Frank lived with.

There is no parallel to be drawn between the two, yet Stevens, eyes now open to the world as it is, also chose to affirm. In a sense, of course, there is no choice. Yet, you choose even if you choose not to. See and choose, or be lost instantly in the chaos. This is true, but there are few who do so, particularly now when any affirmation appears to be the new sentimentality and when the easiest cynicism appears to be the new reality. Yet, Stevens chose to believe in the innate goodness in man. He chose to care. He chose to have faith in Shane and Anne Frank, in Jett Rink and Jesus Christ.

As a director, probably as a man as well, he has always cared. The difference is that now he knows what he is doing when he cares. Earlier, this undifferentiated caring, was responsible for some of his worst excesses. His musical comedies are leaden. Such films are supposed to be free, irresponsible. Stevens always cared too much. He draws closer to the caperings of Astaire and Rogers in the same way as he later draws close to the Crucifixion, hovering, caring. He sits and watches the inanities of Eric Blore just as he sits and watches one of Katharine Hepburn's finest performances, on the edge of his set, as it were, watching, hoping, caring. His comedies are unsuccessful because, caring, he made very slow and careful films. The fact that Stevens could never not care is why he was unable to make light, spontaneous-appearing pictures. When he understood himself well enough to know not to try, he began making those films—those he made after the war—which were his best, those in which he truly expressed himself.

So strong is the character forming these pictures that even had Stevens been allowed to make those he most wanted to—*Paths of Glory, The Naked and the Dead, Winterset,* among them—one doubts that his career would have been any different, that the body of his films would contribute any knowledge or feeling we do not have from the films he actually did make.

Stevens' slowness, his carefulness, his ability to watch, his extraordinary craftsmanship, the fact that he—the least cynical of all motion-picture directors—has always been able to care: these qualities fused to create a series of motion pictures which are much more meaningful to us and our times than is generally admitted.

His attitude is often dismissed as sentimental. Certainly his excesses are often sentimental enough, but his attitude is not invariably so. The attitude, as revealed in the later films is, rather, surprisingly rigorous.

One is finally and fully responsible for one's convictions. These must be evaluated and then put into action. To choose to affirm has nothing weak about it. It is, rather, an act of bravery, which is perhaps the reason one sees it so rarely, and so rarely believes it when one sees it. The way from the safe romantic dilemma is to deny the validity of one's easy subjective interpretation, to affirm a possible objectivity in a world perfectly indifferent to feelings and thoughts alike. There are few romantics who successfully enter this real world —few, certainly, of Stevens' time, and few, absolutely, from America, a country which early in its short history was taught to believe that the reality of today is worthless as compared with the romance of tomorrow, that being is nothing and that becoming is all, a country imbued from its earliest years with a romanticism that

Following page: *Giant*

continues to this day.

Romanticism now continues in America with a difference. It has reached the point where a romantic revolt is possible. It has reached the George Eastman stage, has not yet entered the Shane stage. A degree of self-knowledge is now common knowledge, and this being so, a revolt against civilization as we have known it is in progress. The social schism is ignored. The attack is rightly against the Establishment. Individuals, minorities of one, now band together. The formerly stigmatized strike back. At the same time—and this was George Eastman's problem—never have subjective feelings more rigidly controlled the half-awakened romantic. A thousand hungry and romantic egos are calling out for instant recognition in the arts; a hundred million cry out that they want to be loved for themselves alone. And in the midst of this adolescent turmoil, a growing awareness of the tragic nature of life itself.

All of these are cause and symptom of an enormous romantic crisis, one solution of which could be the sudden and sobering glimpse—probably through war again—of the real world as it really is, leading to that moment of illumination where the subjective turns suddenly objective.

One thinks of the worlds of *Shane, of Giant,* of *A Place in the Sun,* as being far away from our time, and in a sense, so they are. At the same time, they are prophetic, as all art is prophetic. They indicate what can happen, what one hopes will happen, when the American romantic finally realizes himself as a human being.

George Stevens as cameraman

Filmography

George Stevens originally worked as a cameraman for the Hal Roach studios. Among the shorts and features he worked on there were: 1924, *The White Sheep, The Battling Oriole;* 1925, *Black Cyclone;* 1926, *The Devil Horse, The Desert's Toll;* 1927, *No Man's Law, The Valley of Hell, Lightning;* a number of the Laurel and Hardy films—among them, 1926, *Putting Pants on Philip;* 1927, *The Battle of the Century;* 1928, *Leave 'em Laughing, Two Tars, Unaccustomed as We Are;* 1929, *Big Business*—and, in 1930, some of the Harry Langdon shorts. In 1930 Stevens became a director for the Hal Roach studios. Among his shorts were: 1930, *Ladies Past;* 1931, *Call a Cop!, High Gear, The Kick-Off, Mama Loves Papa.* In 1932 he began directing for the Universal studio, where he made such shorts as: 1932, *The Finishing Touch, Boys Will Be Boys, Family Troubles;* 1933, *Should Crooners Marry?, Hunting Trouble, Rock-a-bye Cowboy, Room Mates.* He has also made the following shorts for the RKO studio: 1933, *A Divorce Courtship, Flirting in the Park, Quiet Please, Grin and Bear It;* 1934, *Bridal Bail, Ocean Swells.* In 1933 he made his first feature film.

The Cohens and the Kellys in Trouble. George Sidney, Charlie Murray,
George Stevens

The Cohens and the Kellys in Trouble

Universal Pictures

Director **George Stevens**
Screenplay **Fred Guiol** and **Al Austin** after an original story
by **Homer Croy** and **Vernon Smith** Photography **Len Powers**
Editor **Robert Carlisle** Previewed **March 7, 1933**
Running time **68 minutes**

George Sidney *Nathan Cohen* **Charlie Murray** *Patrick Kelly*
Maureen O'Sullivan *Mollie* **Andy Devine** *Anderson*
Jobyna Howland *Queenie* **Frank Albertson** *Bob Graham*
Maude Fulton *Fern* **Henry Armetta** *Captain Silva*
Arthur Hoyt *Boswell* **Max Davidson** *Larson*
Herbert Corthell *Panhandler* **Olive Cooper** *Swedish Stewardess*
Willie Fong *Ah Chung* **Don Brody** *Chauffeur*
Edward Le Saint *Freighter Captain* **Maurice Black** *Mick*

Bachelor Bait

RKO Radio Pictures

Producer **Lou Brock** Director **George Stevens**
Screenplay **Glenn Tryon** after an original story by **Victor**
and **Edward Halperin** Photography **Dave Abel**
Art Directors **Van Nest Polglase** and **Carroll Clark**
Costumes **Walter Plunkett** Music **Max Steiner**
Editing **James B. Morley** Released **July 27, 1934**
Running time **75 minutes**

Stuart Erwin *Wilber* **Rochelle Hudson** *Linda*
Pert Kelton *Allie* **Skeets Gallagher** *Von*
Berton Churchill *Barney* **Grady Sutton** *Don*
Clarence H. Wilson *District Attorney* **William Augustin**
Hazel Forbes

Kentucky Kernels. "Spanky" McFarland, Robert Woolsey, Bert Wheeler, George Stevens

Kentucky Kernels

RKO Radio Pictures

Producer **H. N.** Swanson Director **George Stevens**
Screenplay **Fred Guiol, Bert Kalmar** and **Harry Ruby**
Photography **Eddie Cronjager**
Music **Bert Kalmar** and **Harry Ruby**
Editor **James Morley** Previewed **October 6, 1934**
Running time **74 minutes**

Bert Wheeler *Willie* **Robert Woolsey** *Elmer*
Mary Carlisle *Gloria* **"Spanky" McFarland** *Spanky*
Noah Beery *Col. Wakefield* **Lucille La Verne** *Hannah Milford*
Sleep 'n' Eat *Buckshot* **William Pawley** **Paul Page**
Roger Gray **Louis Mason** **Frank McGlynn, Jr.**
Richard Alexander

Laddie

RKO Radio Pictures

Producer **Pandro S. Berman** Director **George Stevens**
Screenplay **Ray Harris** and **Dorothy Yost** after the
Gene Stratton Porter novel Photography **Harold Wenstrom**
Art Directors **Van Nest Polglase** and **Perry Ferguson**
Music **Roy Webb** Editor **James Morley**
Released **March 29, 1935**
Running time **70 minutes**

John Beal *Laddie Stanton* **Gloria Stuart** *Pamela Pryor*
Virginia Weidler *Little Sister* **Donald Crisp** *Mr. Pryor*
Dorothy Peterson *Mrs. Stanton*
Willard Robertson *Mr. Stanton*
William Bakewell *Robert Pryor* **Gloria Shea** *Sally Stanton*
Charlotte Henry *Shelly Stanton* **Jimmy Butler** *Leon Stanton*
Grady Sutton *Peter Dover* **Greta Meyer** *Candace*
Mary Forbes *Mrs. Pryor*

The Nitwits

RKO Radio Pictures

Producer **Lee Marcus** Director **George Stevens**
Screenplay **Fred Guiol** and **Al Boasberg** after an original
story by **Stuart Palmer** Photography **Eddie Cronjager**
Art Directors **Van Nest Polglase** and **Perry Ferguson**
Music **Dorothy Fields, Jimmy McHugh, L. Wolfe Gilbert**
and **Felix Bernard** Editor **John Lockert**
Released **June 7, 1935** Running time **81 minutes**

Bert Wheeler *Johnny* **Robert Woolsey** *Newton*
Fred Keating *Darrell* **Betty Grable** *Mary Roberts*
Evelyn Brent *Mrs. Lake* **Erik Rhodes** *Clark*
Hale Hamilton *Mr. Lake* **Charles Wilson** *Capt. Jennings*
Arthur Aylesworth *Lurch* **Willie Best** *Sleepy*
Lew Kelly *J. Gabriel Hazel* **Dorothy Granger** *Phyllis*

Alice Adams

RKO Radio Pictures

Producer **Pandro S. Berman**   Director **George Stevens**
Screenplay **Dorothy Yost, Mortimer Offner** and **Jane Murfin**
after the **Booth Tarkington** novel
Photography **Robert De Grasse**
Art Director **Van Nest Polglase**   Music **Max Steiner**
Previewed **August 2, 1935**   Running time **99 minutes**

Katharine Hepburn *Alice Adams*   **Fred MacMurray** *Arthur Russell*
Fred Stone *Mr. Adams*   **Evelyn Venable** *Mildred Palmer*
Frank Albertson *Walter Adams*   **Ann Shoemaker** *Mrs. Adams*
Charles Grapewin *Mr. Lamb*   **Grady Sutton** *Frank Dowling*
Hedda Hopper *Mrs. Palmer*   **Jonathan Hale** *Mr. Palmer*
Janet McLead *Henrietta Lamb*   **Virginia Howell** *Mrs. Dowling*
Zeffie Tilbury *Mrs. Dresser*   **Ella McKenzie** *Ella Dowling*
Hattie McDaniel *Malena*

Annie Oakley

RKO Radio Pictures

Producer **Cliff Reid**   Director **George Stevens**
Screenplay **Joel Sayre** and **John Twist** after an original
story by **Joseph A. Fields** and **Ewart Adamson**
Photography **J. Roy Hunt**
Art Directors **Van Nest Polglase** and **Perry Ferguson**
Music **Alberto Colombo**   Editor **George Hively**
Previewed **October 25, 1935**   Running time **88 minutes**

Barbara Stanwyck *Annie Oakley*   **Preston Foster** *Toby Taylor*
Melvyn Douglas *Jeff Hogarth*   **Moroni Olsen** *Buffalo Bill*
Pert Kelton *Vera Delmar*   **Andy Clyde** *MacIvor*
Margaret Armstrong *Mrs. Oakley*
Delmar Watson *Wesley Oakley*   **Adeline Craig** *Susan Oakley*
Chief Thunder Bird *Old Sitting Bull*

Swing Time

RKO Radio Pictures

Producer **Pandro S. Berman**   Director **George Stevens**
Screenplay **Howard Lindsay** and **Allan Scott** after an original
story by **Erwin Gelsey**   Photography **David Abel**
Art Directors **Van Nest Polglase, Carroll Clark, John Harkrider**
and **Darrell Silvera**   Costumes **Bernard Newman**
Music **Jerome Kern** and **Dorothy Fields**
Choreography **Hermes Pan**   Editor **Henry Berman**
Previewed **September 27, 1936**   Running time **105 minutes**

Fred Astaire *Lucky*   **Ginger Rogers** *Penny*   **Victor Moore** *Pop*
Helen Broderick *Mabel*   **Eric Blore** *Mr. Gordon*
Betty Furness *Margaret*   **Georges Metaxa** *Ricardo Romero*
John Harrington *Raymond*   **Pierre Watkin** *Simpson*
Landers Stevens *Judge Watson*   **Gerald Homer** *Eric*
Abe Reynolds *Tailor*   **Fern Emmett** *Maid*
Howard Hickman *First Minister*   **Edgar Dearing** *Policeman*
Ferdinand Minuer *Second Minister*   **Olin Francis** *Tough Mug*

Quality Street

RKO Radio Pictures

Producer **Pandro S. Berman**   Director **George Stevens**
Screenplay **Allan Scott** and **Mortimer Offner** after the play by
Sir James M. Barrie   Photography **Robert De Grasse**
Art Director **Hobe Erwin**, with **Darrell Silvera**
Costumes **Walter Plunkett**   Music **Roy Webb**
Editor **Henry Berman**   Previewed **March 5, 1937**
Running time **84 minutes**

Katharine Hepburn *Phoebe Throssel*
Franchot Tone *Dr. Valentine Brown*   **Eric Blore** *Sergeant*
Fay Bainter *Susan Throssel*   **Cora Witherspoon** *Patty*
Estelle Winwood *Mary Willoughby*
Florence Lake *Henrietta Turnbull*
Helena Grant *Fanny Willoughby*   **Bonita Granville** *Isabella*
Clifford Severn *Arthur*   **Sherwood Bailey** *William Smith*
Roland Varno *Ensign Blades*   **Joan Fontaine** *Charlotte Parrett*
William Bakewell *Lt. Spicer*   **York Sherwood** *Postman*

A Damsel in Distress

RKO Radio Pictures

Producer **Pandro S. Berman**   Director **George Stevens**
Screenplay **P. G. Wodehouse, Ernest Pagano** and **S. K. Lauren**
after the **Wodehouse** novel   Photography **Joseph H. August**
Art Directors **Van Nest Polglase** and **Carroll Clark**
Music **George** and **Ira Gershwin**   Choreography **Hermes Pan**
Editor **Henry Berman**   Released **November 19, 1937**
Running time **100 minutes**

Fred Astaire *Jerry*   **George Burns** *Georgie*   **Gracie Allen** *Gracie*
Joan Fontaine *Lady Alyce*   **Reginald Gardiner** *Keggs*
Ray Noble *Reggie*   **Constance Collier** *Lady Caroline*
Montagu Love *Lord Marshmorton*   **Henry Watson** *Albert*
Jan Duggan *Miss Ruggles*

Vivacious Lady

RKO Radio Pictures

Producer and Director **George Stevens**
Screenplay **P. J. Wolfson** and **Ernest Pagano** after a story
by **I. A. R. Wylie**   Photography **Robert De Grasse**
Art Director **Van Nest Polglase**
Costumes **Irene** and **Bernard Newman**   Music **Roy Webb**
Editor **Henry Berman**   Released **May 13, 1938**
Running time **90 minutes**

Ginger Rogers *Francy*   **James Stewart** *Peter*
James Ellison *Keith*   **Beulah Bondi** *Mrs. Morgan*
Charles Coburn *Mr. Morgan*   **Frances Mercer** *Helen*
Phyllis Kennedy *Jenny*   **Grady Sutton** *Culpepper*
Franklin Pangborn *Apartment Manager*   **Alec Craig** *Joseph*
Jack Carson *Waiter Captain*   **Willie Best** *Porter*
Dorothy Moore   **Maurice Black**   **Frank M. Thomas**
Spencer Carters   **Maude Eburne**   **Bobbie Barber**

Gunga Din. Cary Grant, Victor McLaglen, Douglas Fairbanks, Jr., George Stevens

Gunga Din

RKO Radio Pictures

Producer and Director **George Stevens**
Executive Producer **Pandro S. Berman**
Screenplay **Joel Sayre** and **Fred Guiol** after an original story
by **Ben Hecht** and **Charles MacArthur** suggested by the
Rudyard Kipling poem   Photography **Joseph H. August**
Art Directors **Van Nest Polglase** and **Perry Ferguson,** with
Darrell Silvera   Music **Alfred Newman**
Editors **Henry Berman** and **John Lockert**
Released **January 27, 1939**   Running time **117 minutes**

Cary Grant *Cutter*   **Victor McLaglen** *MacChesney*
Douglas Fairbanks, Jr. *Ballantine*   **Sam Jaffe** *Gunga Din*
Eduardo Ciannelli *Sufi Khan*   **Joan Fontaine** *Emmy*
Montagu Love *Col. Weeks*   **Robert Coote** *Higginbotham*
Abner Biberman *Cheta*   **Lumsden Hare** *Major Mitchell*

Vigil in the Night. George Stevens, Carole Lombard

Vigil in the Night

RKO Radio Pictures

Producer and Director **George Stevens**
Screenplay **Fred Guiol, P. J. Wolfson** and **Rowland Leigh** after
the novel by **A. J. Cronin**   Photography **Robert De Grasse**
Music **Alfred Newman**   Editor **Henry Berman**
Released **February 9, 1940**   Running time **96 minutes**

Carole Lombard *Anne Lee*   **Brian Aherne** *Dr. Prescott*
Anne Shirley *Lucy Lee*   **Julien Mitchell** *Mathew Bowley*
Robert Coote *Dr. Caley*   **Brenda Forbes** *Nora*
Rita Page *Glennie*   **Peter Cushing** *Joe Shand*
Ethel Griffies *Matron East*   **Doris Lloyd** *Mrs. Bowley*
Emily Fitzroy *Sister Gilson*

Penny Serenade. Irene Dunne, Cary Grant, George Stevens

Penny Serenade

Columbia Pictures

Producer and Director **George Stevens**
Associate Producer **Fred Guiol**
Screenplay **Morrie Ryskind** after a story by **Martha Cheavens**
Photography **Joseph Walker**   Music **W. Franke Harling**
Editor **Otto Meyer**   Released **April 24, 1941**
Running time **125 minutes**

Irene Dunne *Julie Gardiner*   **Cary Grant** *Roger Adams*
Beulah Bondi *Miss Oliver*   **Edgar Buchanan** *Applejack*
Ann Doran *Dotty*   **Eva Lee Kuney** *Trina—age 6*
Leonard Wiley *Dr. Hartley*   **Wallis Clark** *Judge*
Walter Soderling *Billings*   **Baby Biffle** *Trina—age 1*

Woman of the Year. Spencer Tracy, George Stevens, Katharine Hepburn

Woman of the Year

Metro-Goldwyn-Mayer Pictures

Producer **Joseph L. Mankiewicz**   Director **George Stevens**
Screenplay **Ring Lardner, Jr.**, and **Michael Kanin**
Photography **Joseph Ruttenberg**   Music **Franz Waxman**
Art Director **Cedric Gibbons**, with **Edwin B. Willis**
Editor **Frank Sullivan**   Released **February 1, 1942**
Running time **112 minutes**

Spencer Tracy *Sam Craig*   **Katharine Hepburn** *Tess Harding*
Fay Bainter *Ellen Whitcomb*   **Reginald Owen** *Clayton*
Minor Watson *William Harding*
William Bendix *"Pinkie" Peters*   **Gladys Blake** *Flo Peters*
Dan Tobin *Gerald Howe*   **Roscoe Karns** *Phil Whittaker*
William Tannen *Ellis*   **Ludwig Stossel** *Dr. Lubbeck*
Sara Haden *Matron*   **Edith Evenson** *Alma*
George Kezas *Chris*

The Talk of the Town

Columbia Pictures

Producer and Director **George Stevens**
Associate Producer **Fred Guiol**
Screenplay **Irwin Shaw** and **Sidney Buchman** after an
adaptation of the **Sidney Harmon** story by **Dale Van Every**
Photography **Ted Tetzlaff**
Art Directors **Lionel Banks** and **Rudolph Sternad**
Music **Frederick Hollander**   Editor **Otto Meyer**
Previewed **July 26, 1942**   Running time **118 minutes**

Cary Grant *Leopold Dilg*   **Jean Arthur** *Nora Shelley*
Ronald Colman *Michael Lightcap*   **Edgar Buchanan** *Sam Yeates*
Glenda Farrell *Regina Bush*   **Charles Dingle** *Andrew Holmes*
Emma Dunn *Mrs. Shelley*   **Rex Ingram** *Tilney*
Leonid Kinskey *Jan Pulaski*   **Tom Tyler** *Clyde Bracken*
Don Beddoe *Chief of Police*   **George Watts** *Judge Grunstadt*
Clyde Fillmore *Senator James Boyd*
Frank M. Thomas *District Attorney*

The More the Merrier. Jean Arthur, Charles Coburn, George Stevens

The More the Merrier

Columbia Pictures

Producer and Director **George Stevens**
Associate Producer **Fred Guiol**
Screenplay **Robert Russell, Frank Ross, Richard Flournoy**
and **Lewis R. Foster** after an original story by **Robert Russell**
and **Frank Ross**   Photography **Ted Tetzlaff**
Art Directors **Lionel Banks** and **Rudolph Sternad**
Music **Leigh Harline**   Editor **Otto Meyer**
Released **May 13, 1943**   Running time **104 minutes**

Jean Arthur *Connie Milligan*   **Joel McCrea** *Joe Carter*
Charles Coburn *Benjamin Dingle*
Richard Gaines *Charles J. Pendergast*   **Bruce Bennett** *Evans*
Frank Sully *Pike*   **Clyde Fillmore** *Senator Noonan*
Stanley Clements *Morton Rodakiewicz*   **Don Douglas** *Harding*

I Remember Mama

RKO Radio Pictures

Producer **Harriet Parsons**
Director and Executive Producer **George Stevens**
Screenplay **DeWitt Bodeen** from the **John Van Druten** play
based on the **Kathryn Forbes** novel
Photography **Nicholas Musuraca**
Art Directors **Albert D'Agostino** and **Carroll Clark**, with
Darrell Silvera and **Emile Kuri**
Costumes **Edward Stevenson** and **Gile Steele**
Music **Roy Webb** Editors **Robert Swink** and **Tholen Gladden**
Released **March 13, 1948** Running time **134 minutes**

Irene Dunne *Mama* **Barbara Bel Geddes** *Katrin*
Oscar Homolka *Uncle Chris* **Philip Dorn** *Papa*
Sir Cedric Hardwicke *Mr. Hyde* **Edgar Bergen** *Mr. Thorkelson*
Rudy Vallee *Dr. Johnson* **Barbara O'Neil** *Jessie Brown*
Peggy McIntyre *Christine* **June Hedin** *Dagmar*
Steve Brown *Nels* **Ellen Corby** *Aunt Trina*
Hope Landin *Aunt Jenny* **Edith Evanson** *Aunt Sigrid*
Tommy Ivo *Cousin Arne* **Florence Bates** *Florence Dana Moorhead*

A Place in the Sun. George Stevens, Montgomery Clift, Elizabeth Taylor

The scene as it appeared in the film

A Place in the Sun

Paramount Pictures

Producer and Director **George Stevens**
Associate Producer **Ivan Moffat**
Screenplay **Michael Wilson** and **Harry Brown** after the
Patrick Kearney play based on **Theodore Dreiser's**
An American Tragedy Photography **William C. Mellor**
Art Directors **Hans Dreier** and **Walter Tyler**
Costumes **Edith Head** Music **Franz Waxman**
Editor **William Hornbeck** Released **September 1951**
Running time **122 minutes**

Montgomery Clift *George Eastman*
Elizabeth Taylor *Angela Vickers*
Shelley Winters *Alice Tripp* **Anne Revere** *Hannah Eastman*
Raymond Burr *Marlowe* **Herbert Heyes** *Charles Eastman*
Keefe Brasselle *Earl Eastman*
Shepperd Strudwick *Anthony Vickers*
Frieda Inescort *Mrs. Vickers* **Ian Wolfe** *Dr. Wyeland*
Lois Chartrand *Marsha Eastman* **Fred Clark** *Bellows*
Walter Sande *Jansen* **Douglas Spencer** *Boatkeeper*
John Ridgely *Coroner* **Kathryn Givney** *Mrs. Louise Eastman*
Ted de Corsia *Judge* **Charles Dayton** *Kelly*
Paul Frees *Reverend Morrison* **William Murphy** *Mr. Whiting*

Something to Live For

Paramount Pictures

Producer and Director **George Stevens**
Associate Producer **Ivan Moffat**
Screenplay **Dwight Taylor** Photography **George Barnes**
Art Directors **Hal Pereira** and **Walter Tyler**, with **Emile Kuri**
Costumes **Edith Head** Music **Victor Young**
Editors **William Hornbeck** and **Tom McAdoo**
Released **March 1952** Running time **89 minutes**

Shane. Rehearsing the fight scene. Stevens taking both parts. (See page 65 for scene as it appeared in the film.)

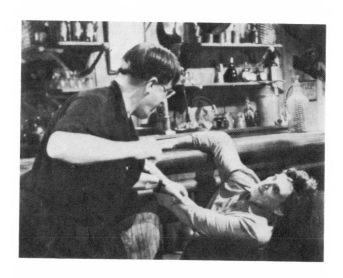

Joan Fontaine *Jenny Carey*   Ray Milland *Alan Miller*
Teresa Wright *Edna Miller*   Richard Derr *Tony Collins*
Douglas Dick *Baker*   Herbert Heyes *Mr. Crawley*
Harry Bellaver *Billy*   Paul Valentine *Albert*
Frank Orth *Waiter*   Bob Cornthwaite *Young Man*
Helen Spring *Mrs. Crawley*   Rudy Lee *Chris Miller*
Patric Mitchell *Johnny Miller*

Shane

Paramount Pictures

Producer and Director **George Stevens**
Associate Producer **Ivan Moffat**
Screenplay **A. B. Guthrie, Jr.**, after the novel by **Jack Schaefer**, with additional dialogue by **Jack Sher**
Photography **Loyal Griggs**
Art Directors **Hal Pereira** and **Walter Tyler**, with **Emile Kuri**
Costumes **Edith Head**   Music **Victor Young**
Editors **William Hornbeck** and **Tom McAdoo**
Released **August 1953**   Running time **118 minutes**

Alan Ladd *Shane*   **Jean Arthur** *Mrs. Starrett*
Van Heflin *Mr. Starrett*   **Brandon de Wilde** *Joey Starrett*
Jack Palance *Wilson*   **Ben Johnson** *Chris*
Edgar Buchanan *Lewis*   **Emile Meyer** *Ryker*
Elisha Cook, Jr. *Torrey*   **Douglas Spencer** *Mr. Shipstead*
John Dierkes *Morgan*   **Ellen Corby** *Mrs. Torry*
Paul McVey *Grafton*   **John Miller** *Atkey*
Edith Evanson *Mrs. Shipstead*   **Leonard Strong** *Wright*
Ray Spiker *Johnson*   **Janice Carroll** *Susan Lewis*
Martin Mason *Howells*   **Nancy Kulp** *Mrs. Howells*
Helen Brown *Mrs. Lewis*

Giant. James Dean, George Stevens.

The scene as it appeared in the film

Giant

Warner Bros. Pictures

Producers **George Stevens** and **Henry Ginsberg**
Director **George Stevens**
Screenplay **Fred Guiol** and **Ivan Moffat** after the novel
by **Edna Ferber**   Photography **William C. Mellor**
Production Designer **Boris Leven,** with **Ralph Hurst**
Costumes **Marjorie Best** and **Moss Mabry**
Music **Dimitri Tiomkin**   Editor **William Hornbeck**
Released **November 24, 1956**   Running time **198 minutes**

Elizabeth Taylor *Leslie Lynnton*   **Rock Hudson** *Bick Benedict*
James Dean *Jett Rink*   **Carroll Baker** *Luz Benedict II*
Jane Withers *Vashti Synthe*   **Chill Wills** *Uncle Bawley*
Mercedes McCambridge *Luz Benedict*
Sal Mineo *Angel Obregon III*
Dennis Hopper *Jordan Benedict III*
Judith Evelyn *Mrs. Horace Lynnton*
Paul Fix *Dr. Horace Lynnton*
Rod Taylor *Sir David Karfrey*   **Earl Holliman** *Bob Dace*
Robert Nichols *Pinky Synthe*   **Alexander Scourby** *Old Polo*
Fran Bennett *Judy Benedict*   **Charles Watts** *Whitside*
Elsa Cardenas *Juana*   **Carolyn Craig** *Lacey Lynnton*
Monte Hale *Bale Clinch*   **Mary Ann Edwards** *Adarene Clinch*
Sheb Wooley *Gabe Target*   **Victor Millan** *Angel Obregon I*
Mickey Simpson *Sarge*   **Pilar del Rey** *Mrs. Obregon*
Maurice Jara *Dr. Guerra*   **Noreen Nash** *Lorna Lane*
Napoleon Whiting *Swazey*   **Tina Menard** *Lupe*
Ray Whitley *Watts*

The Diary of Anne Frank

Twentieth Century-Fox Pictures

Producer and Director **George Stevens**
Associate Producer **George Stevens, Jr.**
Screenplay based on **Anne Frank's** *Diary* and the
dramatization of **Anne Frank's** writings by **Frances Goodrich**
and **Albert Hackett**
Photography **William C. Mellor** and **Jack Cardiff**
Art Directors **Lyle R. Wheeler** and **George W. Davis,**
with **Walter Scott** and **Stuart Reiss**
Costumes **Charles LeMaire** and **Mary Wills**
Music **Alfred Newman**
Editors **David Bretherton, Robert Swink** and **William Mace**
Released **July 1959**   Running time **170 minutes**

Millie Perkins *Anne Frank*   **Joseph Schildkraut** *Otto Frank*
Shelley Winters *Mrs. Van Daan*
Richard Beymer *Peter Van Daan*
Lou Jacobi *Mr. Van Daan*   **Gusti Huber** *Mrs. Frank*
Diane Baker *Margot Frank*   **Douglas Spencer** *Kraler*
Dody Heath *Miep*   **Ed Wynn** *Mr. Dussel*

The Greatest Story Ever Told

United Artists Productions

Producer and Director **George Stevens**
Executive Producer **Frank I. Davis**
Associate Producers **George Stevens, Jr.,** and **Antonio Vellani**
Screenplay **James Lee Barrett** and **George Stevens** after
the Bible and the writings of **Fulton Oursler** and **Henry Denker**
and in creative association with **Carl Sandburg**
Photography **William C. Mellor** and **Loyal Griggs**
Art Directors **Richard Day** and **William Creber**, with **David Hall**
Costumes **Vittorio Nino Novarese** and **Marjorie Best**
Music **Alfred Newman**

Editor **Harold F. Kress**, with **Argyle Nelson, Jr.**, and
Frank O'Neill Released **February 15, 1965**
Running time **210 minutes**

Max von Sydow *Jesus* **Dorothy McGuire** *Mary*
Robert Loggia *Joseph* **Charlton Heston** *John the Baptist*
Michael Anderson, Jr. *James the Younger*
Robert Blake *Simon the Zealot* **Burt Brinckerhoff** *Andrew*
John Considine *John* **Jamie Farr** *Thaddaeus*
Peter Mann *Nathanael* **David McCallum** *Judas Iscariot*
Roddy McDowall *Matthew* **Gary Raymond** *Peter*
David Sheiner *James the Elder* **Ina Balin** *Martha of Bethany*
Janet Margolin *Mary of Bethany* **Michael Tolan** *Lazarus*
Sidney Poitier *Simon of Cyrene*
Joanna Dunham *Mary Magdalene* **Carroll Baker** *Veronica*
Pat Boone *Young Man at the Tomb*
Van Heflin *Bar Amand* **Sal Mineo** *Uriah*
Shelley Winters *Woman of No Name* **Ed Wynn** *Old Aram*
John Wayne *The Centurion* **Telly Savalas** *Pontius Pilate*
Angela Lansbury *Claudia* **David Hedison** *Philip*
Johnny Seven *Pilate's Aide* **Tom Reese** *Thomas*
Paul Stewart *Questor* **Harold J. Stone** *General Varus*
Martin Landau *Caiaphas* **Nehemiah Persoff** *Shemiah*
Joseph Schildkraut *Nicodemus* **Victor Buono** *Sorak*
Robert Busch *Emissary* **John Crawford** *Alexander*
Russell Johnson *Scribe* **John Lupton** *Speaker of Capernaum*
Abraham Sofaer *Joseph of Arimathaea* **Chet Stratton** *Theophilus*
Ron Whelan *Annas* **Jose Ferrer** *Herod Antipas*
Claude Rains *Herod the Great* **John Abbott** *Aben*
Rodolfo Acosta *Captain of Lancers*
Michael Ansara *Herod's Commander* **Philip Coolidge** *Chuza*
Dal Jenkins *Philip* **Joe Perry** *Archelaus*
Marian Seldes *Herodias* **Richard Conte** *Barabbas*
Donald Pleasence *The Dark Hermit*
Frank De Kova *The Tormentor* **Joseph Sirola** *Dumah*
Cyril Delevanti *Melchior* **Mark Leonard** *Balthazar*
Frank Silvera *Caspar*

The Only Game in Town

Twentieth Century-Fox Pictures in association with
George Stevens Films, Ltd.

Producer **Fred Kohlmar**   Director **George Stevens**
Screenplay **Frank Gilroy** based on his play
Photography **Henri Decae**
Art Directors **Herman Blumenthal** and **August Capelier**
Costumes **Mia Fonssagrives** and **Vicky Tiel**
Music **Maurice Jarre**
Editors **John W. Holmes, William Sands** and **Pat Shade**
Released **1970**   Running time **112 minutes**

Elizabeth Taylor *Fran Walker*   **Warren Beatty** *Joe Grady*
Charles Braswell *Thomas J. Lockwood*   **Hank Henry** *Tony*

Awards

George Stevens and his films have won the following prizes: 1936, *Swing Time,* Academy Award for "Best Song"— "The Way You Look Tonight"; 1942, *Woman of the Year,* Academy Award for "Best Screenplay, Original" to Ring Lardner, Jr., and Michael Kanin; 1943, *The More the Merrier,* Academy Award for "Best Supporting Actor" to Charles Coburn, George Stevens nominated for "Best Director"; 1951, *A Place in the Sun,* Academy Awards—"Best Direction" to George Stevens, "Best Costume Design" to Edith Head, "Best Cinematography" to William C. Mellor, "Best Music Score" to Franz Waxman, "Best Screenplay" to Michael Wilson and Harry Brown—George Stevens also received the Screen Directors Guild Award; 1953, *Shane,* Academy Award for "Best Cinematography, Color" to Loyal Griggs, the Irving G. Thalberg Memorial Award from the Academy of Motion Picture Arts and Sciences to George Stevens, also nominated for "Best Direction" Academy Award, and Screen Directors Guild Award; 1956, *Giant,* Academy Award for "Best Direction" and Screen Directors Guild Award to George Stevens; 1959, *The Diary of Anne Frank,* Academy Awards for "Best Supporting Actress" to Shelley Winters, "Best Art Direction" to Lyle R. Wheeler and George W. Davis, "Best Cinematography, Black-and-White" to William C. Mellor, George Stevens nominated for "Best Direction" Academy Award, and Screen Directors Guild Award.

Trustees of The Museum of Modern Art

Chairman of the Board **David Rockefeller**
Vice Chairman **Henry Allen Moe**
Vice Chairman **John Hay Whitney**
Vice Chairman **Gardner Cowles**
President **William S. Paley**
Vice President **James Thrall Soby**
Vice President **Mrs. Bliss Parkinson**
Treasurer **Willard C. Butcher**

Walter Bareiss **Robert R. Barker** *****Alfred H. Barr, Jr.**
William A. M. Burden **J. Frederic Byers, III**
Ivan Chermayeff *****Mrs. W. Murray Crane** **John de Menil**
Mrs. C. Douglas Dillon **Mrs. Edsel B. Ford**
*****Mrs. Simon Guggenheim** **George Heard Hamilton**
*****Wallace K. Harrison** *****Mrs. Walter Hochschild**
*****James W. Husted** **Philip Johnson** **Mrs. Frank Y. Larkin**
Mrs. Albert D. Lasker **John L. Loeb**
*****Ranald H. Macdonald** *****Mrs. G. Macculloch Miller**
Mrs. Charles S. Payson **Gifford Phillips**
Mrs. John D. Rockefeller 3rd **Nelson A. Rockefeller**
Mrs. Wolfgang Schoenborn **Mrs. Bertram Smith**
Mrs. Donald B. Straus **Walter N. Thayer**
*****Edward M. M. Warburg** *****Monroe Wheeler**

Secretary **Richard H. Koch**
Assistant Treasurer **Sarah Rubenstein**
Assistant Treasurer **Neal J. Farrell**
Assistant Secretary **Miriam G. Cedarbaum**

*Honorary Trustee for Life

Titles in This Series

1.
Roy Armes. Patterns of Realism. 1971

2.
Iris Barry. D. W. Griffith: American Film Master: with an annotated list of films by Eileen Bowser. 1965
bound with
Richard Griffith. Samuel Goldwyn: The Producer and His Films. 1956

3.
Ingmar Bergman. Four Screenplays: Smiles of a Summer Night, The Seventh Seal, Wild Strawberries, The Magician. 1960

4.
Luis Bunuel. Three Screenplays: Viridiana, The Exterminating Angel, Simon of the Desert. 1969

5.
Jean Cocteau. Cocteau on the Film. 1954

6.
Bosley Crowther. The Lion's Share. 1957

7.
Cecil B. DeMille. The Autobiography of Cecil B. DeMille. 1959

8.
Denis Gifford. The British Film Catalogue, 1895–1970. 1973
9.
Abel Green and Joe Laurie, Jr. Show Biz from Vaude to Video. 1951
10.
Robert M. Henderson. D. W. Griffith: His Life and Work. 1972
11.
Charles Higham. Hollywood Cameramen. 1970
12.
Ian C. Jarvie. Movies and Society. 1970
13.
John Howard Lawson. Film in the Battle of Ideas. 1953
14.
John Howard Lawson. Theory and Technique of Playwriting and Screenwriting. Revised edition. 1949
15.
Michael F. Mayer. Foreign Films on American Screens. 1965
16.
Vladimir Nilsen. The Cinema as a Graphic Art. 1959
17.
Robert Richardson. Literature and Film. 1969
18.
Donald Richie. George Stevens: An American Romantic. 1970
19.
Lillian Ross. Picture. 1952
20.
Roberto Rossellini. The War Trilogy: Open City, Paisan, Germany—Year Zero. 1973
21.
Robert Rossen. Three Screenplays: All the King's Men, The Hustler, Lilith. 1972

22.
Mack Sennett. King of Comedy. 1954

23.
Albert E. Smith, with Phil A. Koury. Two Reels and a Crank. 1952

24.
Bob Thomas. Selznick. 1970

25.
Bob Thomas. Thalberg: Life and Legend. 1969

26.
Parker Tyler. Chaplin: Last of the Clowns. 1948

27.
Parker Tyler. The Hollywood Hallucination. 1944

28.
Parker Tyler. Magic and Myth of the Movies. 1947

29.
Luchino Visconti. Two Screenplays: La Terra Trema, Senso. 1970

30.
Luchino Visconti. Three Screenplays: White Nights, Rocco and His Brothers, The Job. 1970

Carson

St. Louis Community College
at Meramec
Library